CHRIST'S PASSION

CHRIST'S PASSION

THE POWER AND THE PROMISE

D. JAMES KENNEDY
WITH JERRY NEWCOMBE

Coral Ridge Ministries
Fort Lauderdale, Florida

CONTENTS

INTRODUCTION

RARELY HAS A MOTION PICTURE stirred the passions of so many before its release as has Mel Gibson's *The Passion of The Christ*. We heard about the film, both pro and con, for months. Many commentators found it interesting to note that the most vociferous critics were usually those who had not seen it. With the scandalous anti-Christian film *The Last Temptation of Christ*, we were warned, "Don't judge it until you see it." Well, I did see it, and it was worse than could be imagined. However, this time someone from Hollywood made a pro-Christian film, and opponents tried various ploys to prevent us from seeing it. So goes "don't judge it until you see it" in our politically correct age.

Mel Gibson's film is incredibly powerful. Viewing it proved to be one of the most intense experiences of my life. If the actual crucifixion could be filmed, I am not sure it would be much different than what Gibson has so expertly put on the screen. This is not only a movie; I am convinced this is a powerful tool that God will use for decades to draw many into His Kingdom. As co-author Jerry Newcombe says: "*The Passion of The Christ* by Mel Gibson is more than just a movie. It is an event."

The purpose of this book is to complement the film and to take an in-depth look at Christ's passion. My goal is to provide supplemental information and the historical backdrop. The film will doubtless raise many questions. It is my goal to answer these questions and more.

This book looks at Christ's passion from several different angles. As we meditate on the incredible price Jesus paid for our redemption, it moves us to love Him that much more.

Beginning in Part I, I deal with the prelude to the passion. Included is a look at how the passion was foretold by Hebrew prophets hundreds of years before Christ was even born.

Part II examines the passion of Christ, including a look at the bitter cup He drank on our behalf. Included in this section is a reverential walk down the Via Dolorosa, the way of sorrows, where we briefly meet some of the key characters of the passion.

In Part III, we meet the key personalities in the passion. Some are presented in their own voice—speaking with candor, sometimes bitterness, about their roles in the crucifixion of Christ.

The final section, Part IV, deals with the power and the promise of the passion. Specifically, I look at the overwhelming evidence for Christ's resurrection from the dead, including a witness from science. I also look at the significance of His passion and resurrection on how we live our lives.

It is my prayer that this book will draw you closer to Jesus. I pray that the details of our Savior's suffering on our behalf will encourage you to serve Him with greater fervor.

—D. James Kennedy, Ph.D.

PART I

THE PRELUDE TO
THE PASSION

CHAPTER 1

BORN TO DIE

All who dwell on the earth will worship him, whose names have not been written in the Book of Life of the Lamb slain from the foundation of the world. If anyone has an ear, let him hear.

REVELATION 13:8-9

HAVE YOU EVER ASKED CHILDREN what they wanted to be when they get older? "Well, tell me, Susie, what do you want to be when you grow up?"

"Oh, I'm going to be an astronaut."

"And how about you, Bobby?"

"I'm going to be the President of the United States."

"And how about you, Johnny?"

"I'm going to be a major league baseball player."

"And how about you, Jesus? What do you plan to be when you grow up?"

The answer: "Dead. That's what I plan to be when I grow up, because, you see, that is why I was born. I was born to die."

There was a higher reason for His having been born to die. Christ came to be a king. Not just "King of the Jews" as was written on the Cross, but He came to be the King of kings and the Lord of lords. In order for Him to achieve this, it was necessary for Him to die. Thus, in one sense He was born to die.

A DECISION MADE IN ETERNITY

You see, everyone was born for something—to be a doctor, lawyer,

3

teacher, minister . . . a thousand other things—except Jesus. Jesus was born for the specific purpose of dying. Unlike every other child who has ever been born and who was born to live, Jesus Christ was born to die. That was a decision made long ago in eternity. Revelation tells us that He was the Lamb slain before the foundation of the earth. Before God ever created the Milky Way or the Andromeda galaxy or spun the nebulae out into space, Jesus Christ was slain in the mind of God—crucified before the foundation of the world. He came to die in order that we might not have to. He came to die because we deserve to die. He came to pay the penalty He alone could pay.

His was the most amazing birth in all of history, because it was not merely a birth. This was an incarnation, as the ever-living God became incarnate in human flesh. God Incarnate. The word "incarnate" is not a word common to the vocabulary of most Americans today; but they probably would recognize chili con carni, which means, of course, chili (usually made with beans); con, "with,"; and carni, "flesh." So God Incarnate means God in human flesh. The great foundational belief of the Christian religion all over the world is that two thousand or so years ago, the Almighty and Eternal God came and walked among us as a human being. This little planet was visited by the great God Almighty.

THE UNIQUENESS OF CHRIST

Christ's birth was unique. There is none other that even claimed to be God. No one claims that Mohammed is God incarnate, or that Confucius was, or Lao-tse, or Zoroaster, or Buddha, or any of the others. Only Christ is the unique God incarnate. Nor does any other religion claim that its founder died for the sins of the world. Only Christ, by His atonement, paid for the sins of mankind. There is no other Savior. Only He took upon Himself our guilt and our sin.

He is unique in His birth, He is unique in His death, and He is unique in His resurrection. No other religion claims that its founder rose from the dead. They are gone forever, they have died, they have passed into corruption, and they have turned to dust and ashes. But Jesus Christ rose again. He is the only one who could say, "I am He who lives, and was dead, and behold, I am alive forevermore" (Revelation 1:18a), and "Because I live, you [who trust in me] will live also" (John 14:19b). He is not only unique in His birth, His incarnation, His atonement, and His resurrection, but He is also unique in His free salvation, which He offers to humankind.

The angel on the first Christmas night said, I "bring you good tidings of great joy," . . . that "there is born to you this day . . . a Savior" (Luke 2:10-11). A Savior is one who dies to save His people from their sins. So what the angels actually said is, "there is born to you this day a 'Die-er.'"

BORN, DIED

Every Sabbath morning at Coral Ridge Presbyterian Church we confess the oldest and most widely accepted of all of the Christian creeds, which, of course, is the Apostles' Creed. In that creed many people often don't realize what they are saying, having confessed that *we believe in God the Father Almighty, maker of heaven and earth* [we say], *and Jesus Christ, his only Son, our Lord, who was* [note well] *conceived by the Holy Ghost, born of the Virgin Mary, suffered under Pontius Pilate, was crucified, dead, and buried.* Born. Died. He was born to die. In comparison with His atoning death, all of the other glorious, marvelous, wonderful things He did pale into relative insignificance.

The Judge of all the Earth must do rightly, we are told, and yet the world is filled with sin. All men have violated the law of God in every conceivable way. We have transgressed His commandments. The Scripture makes it plain that "all have sinned and fall short of the glory of God" (Romans 3:23).

The tragedy, of course, is that our memories are so poor that we do not recall it. How many sins can you remember from ten years ago this day? How many words can you remember from twenty years ago this day? How many deeds from thirty years ago? The truth of the matter is that you don't remember. Consequently, people do not remember their sins. Therefore, they frequently think they are doing quite well. However, as someone put it very aptly: A clear conscience is most frequently the result of a poor memory.

God knows every thought you ever had. You don't, but He does. God knows every word you have ever spoken—every cruel word, every unkind word, every blasphemous word. He said He would "not hold him guiltless who takes His name in vain" (Deuteronomy 5:11). Every lie, every falsehood, every deceit, every bit of hatred that has filled your heart, every lust, every greed, every animosity—all of our sins are known to Him.

CUR DEUS HOMO

Have you ever heard the Latin phrase, *Cur Deus Homo? Deus,* of course, means "God." *Homo,* of course, refers to "man." But *cur?* Dog? No. That means "why." Therefore, we have "Why God man?," which happens to be the title of one of the greatest Christian classics, written 900 years ago by Saint Anselm, the Archbishop of Canterbury. Why did God become man?

Was it because we needed a perfect example? Why was it necessary that the infinitely glorious, omnipotent Creator of the universe, who fashioned the galaxies, should step out of His ivory palace into the filth of a stable and become man?

"If we could but see God, we would know how we ought to live" said Socrates. Philosophers worshiped truth, goodness, and beauty and felt that if only man could see perfect truth and perfect goodness and perfect beauty, he would immediately know how he ought to live his life and would gladly and delightedly follow in that path.

So, one day Truth descended from Heaven and became incarnate in Jesus of Nazareth, who is the Way, the Truth and the Life. He is truth incarnate and goodness, as well, for in Him there was found no sin. He is the Altogether Lovely One, the Rose of Sharon, the Lily of the Valley, the Delightful One, and the Perfect One in whom all is in perfect symmetry. Every quality of human virtue was in perfect balance in Him.

He came and walked among us, and when we saw Him . . . WE HATED HIM! With rough hands we took Him and threw Him on the ground and nailed Him to a Cross, because He was a mirror that showed us our wrinkles and our warts and our ugliness and our sin. We nailed Him to a tree, and then we buried Him in the ground—out of sight and out of mind.

Socrates knew little or nothing about the true depths of the depravity of the human heart. No. Our condition requires something far greater than a perfect exemplar like Christ. That is not the ultimate reason *Cur Deus Homo*.

MORE THAN A GREAT TEACHER

You hear people say, "Oh, Jesus was a great teacher. That is why He came . . . to teach us." There is no doubt that He was not only a great teacher, He was the greatest Teacher who ever taught. He was the paragon of pedagogic expertise.

I think of one skeptic who set about to write a book in which he was going to debunk Christ and get rid of the idea of His deity. As he began to do his research and to read about this One, he was astonished right at the very beginning. He read about this man

- who was born in a stable,
- who lived in a country bumpkin town that was a byword for backwardness: "Can anything good come out of Nazareth?" (John 1:46),
- who never went to school, who never learned—"How does this Man know letters, having never studied?" (John 7:15),
- who never went to college or a university,
- who never had a degree,
- who never traveled, and

- who then emerged out of total obscurity, walked up on a mountain and delivered the most monumental discourse on human ethics the world had ever heard.

The skeptic was stunned. How can this be? So stunned, indeed, was he that the hardened veneer of his unbelief began to crack, and soon he bowed the knee before Christ.

Yes, Christ was the greatest Teacher who ever lived. Let me sum up His teaching for you—bring it all down to the bottom line—and in one sentence tell you the very essence of what Jesus taught, because surely you want to know what is the essence of the teaching of the greatest Teacher who ever lived. Here it is—the culmination of the teaching of Jesus Christ: "Therefore you shall be perfect, just as your Father in heaven is perfect" (Matthew 5:48). Thus He stripped us bare of all of our subterfuges and left us naked before God in all of our iniquity. In short, we don't have an excuse anymore, now that we know. The teaching of Jesus Christ condemns us one and all.

SIN DEMANDS AN INFINITE PENALTY

Our condition demands a far more radical cure than education can provide, which brings us to what Saint Anselm taught us: God became man because the sin of man is an infinite sin. He was not merely referring to the fact that if you take the tens upon tens of thousands of sins in thought and word and deed, of omission and commission, these sins would be piled up over the heads of every one of us. Then, if we added them all together into a gigantic mountain, it would be almost infinite in nature. But Saint Anselm was talking about more than that; he was talking about the fact that the least sin against an infinitely holy Being, such as God, demands an infinite penalty.

I tremble when I think that to take the name of Christ blasphemously is to invite upon one's head an infinite and eternal wrath. God's name should never be taken in vain. When the scribes in the Old Testament copied the Scriptures and they came to any of the names of

God, they paused, they knelt and prayed, and then they wrote that name. But when they came to the *Tetragrammaton,* to that word *Yahweh,* which we spell as Jehovah, the great ultimate name of God Almighty, they laid aside their pen, took off their clothes, bathed, put on clean clothes, took a new pen, dipped it into ink, and with much prayer, wrote the four letters of *Yahweh,* Jehovah.

Today the name of God is bandied about and falls trippingly from the lips of blasphemers everywhere in this society. It is broadcast in our motion pictures and television and radio daily. My soul trembles for such who have committed such infinite offenses against an infinite God and have brought an infinite penalty upon their heads. "You shall not take the name of the LORD your God in vain, for the LORD will not hold him guiltless who takes His name in vain" (Exodus 20:7). The sin of man is an infinite sin because our very nature is corrupt.

Therefore, said Saint Anselm, it demands an infinite payment. Since the penalty must match the crime, there must be an infinite payment made for infinite sin.

However, it is man who has sinned—not a lamb or a bull or a goat. All of the bulls and lambs that died upon a thousand altars of antiquity could never pay for the slightest sins of man. These were all foreshadows of Christ's once and for all sacrifice. It is man who sinned; it is man who must pay. But how can man, who is finite, ever pay an infinite penalty? One way is that he spends an infinite amount of time doing so in Hell. Is there another way? How, in the short space of this world could any man pay such a penalty?

I read a fascinating story about what is, without doubt, the most popular sport in the world. I speak not of football, basketball, or baseball, as we know them, but of soccer. If you go to Europe or South America, you will learn the truth of that statement. They have stadiums there that dwarf the largest of our football stadiums, where people will gather to watch a soccer match, and they go wild.

In this story there was a world cup—a final championship—being played that year in Argentina between Argentina and Brazil. The game was tied until the very last second, when one of the referees made an obviously erroneous call that led to victory for Argentina. The Brazilian fans were not amused, to say the least.

But time went on, months went by, another year came, and another championship was scheduled between the same two teams—this time played in Brazil. The stadium was crowded with 300,000 people—and at least 200,000 were Brazilians. Just to show that they were not unhappy, one wealthy Brazilian had donated a large sum of money to print the most beautiful large programs they had ever seen, done in glossy colors. They just shone. It was a magnificent piece of work.

The game was very close again. In fact, the score was tied down to the very final seconds. The same referee made an obviously false call again. At a prearranged signal, all the Brazilians lifted their programs. Like mirrors, the glossy covers focused the rays of the sun, and 200,000 mirrors focused their light upon that referee, who went poof, and disappeared in a puff of smoke . . . at least so the story went.

I thought to myself that that is precisely what would happen to any mere finite mortal who endeavored to pay an infinite payment. He would simply disappear instantly. He would be extinguished. What was needed was an infinite man: Jesus Christ—the God-man, the *Theanthropos*, and the Creator/creature—joined forever.

CHRIST PAID IT ALL

Christ went to that cruel hill called Golgotha, soaked with the blood of criminals and scattered with the bones of miscreants, murderers, and the off-scouring of the human race. There they laid Him on the Cross. They took spikes and with hammers began to pound them through His flesh. Dear one, those blows ringing down through the corridors of the centuries have awakened countless souls that were asleep in their sins to the deadly peril of their condition. Those blows have smashed and broken the hard hearts of many sinners and caused them to yield themselves to the Savior.

That Cross was set up in place, and then 200,000 billion trillion suns focused, as it were, the wrath of God into the very core and soul of the God-man there upon that Cross, and Christ suffered in body and soul an infinite wrath, an infinite penalty.

The penalty ultimately was paid in full, and the forgiveness of God could be freely proffered to all who would believe, to all who would cast themselves before that Cross and invite the Savior to come into their hearts. That execrable place of Calvary, of Golgotha—that horrible, bloodstained hill—became the place where the Rose of Sharon blossomed, and a fountain was opened that brings cleansing and life eternal to all who will trust in Him alone for their salvation.

Have you received Him? Has that Rose blossomed in your heart? Have you trusted in Him alone as your Savior? Have you repented of your sins and cast yourself before Him saying, "O Lord Jesus, I am the sinner for whom You have suffered so much. Thank you for Your passion and suffering for my sake. Have mercy upon me and forgive me. Come, I yield myself to You. Set up Your throne in my heart and be my Savior and my God. Henceforth, it is my great delight to follow You. Lord, I surrender my life to You. Take me and make me wholly Yours. In Your holy name I pray. Amen."

If you prayed that prayer in sincerity, you have begun the greatest adventure on which you could ever embark. I would strongly urge you to begin to read the Bible every day and to pray. If you have never read the Bible before, start with the Gospel of John (the fourth book of the New Testament).

I also urge you to get involved with a Bible-based, Bible-believing church. If you would like a free book to help you become established in the Christian faith, write to me and ask for *Beginning Again*.[1]

Once we know Jesus as our personal Lord and Savior, our "thank you" to Him for His gift of salvation will be to serve Him in every area of our lives. Good works will naturally flow from our lives, as good apples grow naturally on a good apple tree.

FORGIVENESS THROUGH HIS PASSION

Jesus Christ made forgiveness from God the Father possible because He paid the penalty for our sins. Therefore, we can (and are commanded) to forgive others. "Forgive us our debts as we forgive our debtors" (Matthew 6:12).

In Mel Gibson's film, *The Passion of The Christ*, there is a poignant scene—a flashback to an earlier, well-known incident found in John, chapter 8. There was a woman caught in adultery. The religious leaders prepared to stone her to death—the penalty for this sin, according to the Law of Moses. They asked Jesus about it, in order to trap Him. "This they said, testing Him, that they might have something of which to accuse Him" (John 8:6). At first, Jesus did not answer them, but He kept writing something in the sand—exactly what, we do not know, for the Scriptures don't tell us. But they kept pressing Him, so finally He answered, "He who is without sin among you, let him throw a stone at her first" (v. 7). Then He stooped down and kept writing in the sand. Suddenly, all of the accusers dropped their stones—the older ones first—and they all crept away.

Soon the only ones left there were Jesus and the woman. "He said to her, 'Woman, where are those accusers of yours? Has no one condemned you?' (v. 10).

"She said, 'No one, Lord.'

"And Jesus said to her, 'Neither do I condemn you; go and sin no more'" (v. 11). Here He showed His great compassion.

The compassion of Christ was seen in His passion (the very word from which "compassion" comes). Christ is the very essence of compassion, for He came to endure that passion. All our sorrows, sicknesses, sadness, sins, and all of our transgressions would be heaped on Him there upon that Cross in the bright noonday sun, and He would endure the wrath of God Almighty in our place. He came to suffer; He came to endure that passion and was touched with all of the feeling of our infirmities.

Our salvation has been made possible only by what Jesus Christ

has done. The twelfth century hymn by Saint Bernard of Clairvaux put
it so well:

> What Thou, my Lord, hast suffered,
>   Was all for sinners' gain;
> Mine, Mine was the transgression,
>   But Thine the deadly pain:
> Lo, here I fall, my Savior!
>   'Tis I deserve Thy place;
> Look upon me with Thy favor,
>   Vouchsafe to me Thy grace.
> What language shall I borrow
>   To thank Thee, dearest Friend,
> For this Thy dying sorrow,
>   Thy pity without end?
> O make me Thine forever;
>   And should I fainting be
> Lord, let me never, never
>   Outlive my love for Thee.[2]

THE PASSION OF CHRIST ACCORDING TO THE PROPHETS

For dogs have surrounded Me;
The congregation of the wicked has enclosed Me.
They pierced My hands and My feet.

PSALM 22:16

ONE DAY, MANY YEARS AGO, my wife could not resist. She purchased one of those "scandal rags" they sell by the checkout counters at the grocery stores. You know, the kind that report on the latest Hollywood gossip or scream out absurd, impossible headlines, like: "Crocodile gives birth to normal human baby!" The particular issue she purchased caught her eye because she knew I was interested in prophecies—biblical prophecies. Perhaps this magazine could provide an interesting contrast between prophecies in the Scriptures and today's "oracles."

This was at the beginning of the year, and the issue promised many predictions by our leading psychics and seers as to what would take place that year. So after she brought it home and we read it, we decided to monitor the happenings of that year to see how many, if any, of the dozens of predictions made would come to be. By the end of the year, not one single prophecy was even remotely fulfilled.

What an incredible contrast that is to the life of Jesus Christ. With Him, 333 specific prophecies which contain 456 details were foretold centuries before He came. In this chapter, we want to explore some of these—in particular, as they relate to the passion, that is, His suffering. His passion was most clearly told hundreds of years before He was even born.

There is nothing like this in any other religion. There are twenty-six volumes which claim to be divine scriptures, or their followers claim them to be divine (since many of them make no such claim themselves), yet they contain no specific predictive prophecies. However, the Old Testament has many specific predictions which Jesus of Nazareth fulfilled.

For about a thousand years the prophets of Israel had predicted the coming Messiah, an eternal King, to rule the people. Their prophecies were both specific and memorable.

Consider some of the prophecies we have in the Bible that were predicted in the Old Testament and fulfilled by Jesus in the New Testament. We begin with the first book of the Bible. Speaking to the serpent who tempted Adam and Eve to fall, God states in Genesis 3:15,

> And I will put enmity
> Between you and the woman,
> And between your seed and her Seed;
> He shall bruise your head,
> And you shall bruise His heel.

In Mel Gibson's movie, *The Passion of The Christ,* when Satan appears to tempt Jesus in the Garden of Gethsemane, he releases a snake that slithers toward Jesus (prostrate on the ground in prayer). Christ stands up and forcefully crushes the serpent's head with His heel. This is a symbolic acting out of this Scripture.

Note also about this prophecy that this is the only mention of the seed of a woman in the entire Bible; it is always the seed of a man, it is always the child of a man. In this case it was the seed of the woman, because Christ had no human father.

Here are many other prophecies Jesus fulfilled:

- He would come from the line of Abraham.
- He would come from the line of Judah, of the line of Isaac and that of Jacob.
- He would be from the house of David.
- He would be born of a virgin.
- He would be given the throne of David—a throne that would be an everlasting throne.
- His name would be called Immanuel.
- He would have a forerunner who would proclaim His coming.
- He would be born in Bethlehem, and not merely any Bethlehem, because there were, in fact, two. He would be born in Bethlehem Ephrathah, which was the small Bethlehem down south in Judea. There was a Bethlehem Zebulun in the northern extreme of Israel.
- He would be worshiped by wise men and presented with gifts.
- He would live for a while in Egypt.
- He would be called back from Egypt by His Father.
- His birthplace, Bethlehem, would suffer a massacre of infants (as Herod slaughtered the infants when he heard of the birth of Jesus).
- He would be called a Nazarene.
- He would be zealous for His Father's House.

All of these things were written hundreds of years before He was born. Stop and think, my friends. Suppose you were trying to describe the man who would be inaugurated President of the United States in the year 2764. He was going to be born in a small town—let's say in Mississippi—a town so small it wasn't even on the maps of that day, but it existed. You would have to describe all of his lineage and all of the things he would do and would have done to him during his lifetime. As in Christ's case:

- He would be filled as no other person with God's Spirit.
- He would miraculously heal many.
- The blind would see.
- The deaf would hear.
- The lame would walk.
- He would draw the Gentiles to Himself.
- He would speak in parables.
- He would be rejected by His own family and friends.
- He would make a triumphal entry into Jerusalem.
- He would be praised by little children.
- He would be rejected as a cornerstone of the nation, which He would turn out to be.
- His miracles would not be believed.
- A friend would betray him for a specific amount of money—30 pieces of silver. (This President who shall reign in 2764 shall be betrayed by a friend for how much money? Do you know? How did the prophet know?)
- He would be a man of sorrows, acquainted with grief.
- He would be forsaken by all of His followers.
- He would be scourged and spat upon.
- The money for His betrayal would be used to buy a potter's field.
- He would be crucified between two thieves.
- He would be given gall and vinegar to drink.
- He would suffer the piercing of His hands and feet.
- His garments would be parted among His crucifiers and would be gambled for.
- He would be surrounded and ridiculed by His enemies.
- He would thirst.
- He would commend His spirit to God the Father.
- Not a bone of His body would be broken.
- He would be stared at in death.
- He would be buried with the rich and raised from the dead.

- He would ascend to Heaven.
- He would become a high priest greater than Aaron.
- He would be seated at God's right hand.
- He would become a smiting scepter.
- He would rule the Gentiles.

THE PASSION ACCORDING TO ISAIAH

One of the most remarkable passages of the Old Testament, which speaks so clearly about Jesus Christ, is Isaiah 53. I think it is interesting that this passage is virtually never read in a synagogue today. Why? Because it so evidently points to Jesus Christ that it is an embarrassment to read it. I hope you will read it and familiarize yourself with it. Consider the fact that this was written about 700 B.C. Here is that chapter *in toto*:

¹Who has believed our report?
And to whom has the arm of the LORD been revealed?
²For He shall grow up before Him as a tender plant,
And as a root out of dry ground.
He has no form or comeliness;
And when we see Him,
There is no beauty that we should desire Him.
³He was despised and rejected by men,
A Man of sorrows and acquainted with grief.
And we hid, as it were, our faces from Him;
He was despised, and we did not esteem Him.
⁴Surely He has borne our griefs
And carried our sorrows;
Yet we esteemed Him stricken,
Smitten by God, and afflicted.
⁵But He was wounded for our transgressions,
He was bruised for our iniquities;
The chastisement for our peace was upon Him,

And by His stripes we are healed.

⁶All we like sheep have gone astray;

We have turned, every one, to his own way;

And the Lord has laid on Him the iniquity of us all.

⁷He was oppressed and He was afflicted,

Yet He opened not His mouth;

He was led as a lamb to the slaughter,

And as a sheep before its shearers is silent,

So He opened not His mouth.

⁸He was taken from prison and from judgment,

And who will declare His generation?

For He was cut off from the land of the living;

For the transgressions of My people He was stricken.

⁹And they made His grave with the wicked—

But with the rich at His death,

Because He had done no violence,

Nor was any deceit in His mouth.

¹⁰Yet it pleased the Lord to bruise Him;

He has put Him to grief.

When You make His soul an offering for sin,

He shall see His seed, He shall prolong His days,

And the pleasure of the Lord shall prosper in His hand.

¹¹He shall see the labor of His soul, and be satisfied.

By His knowledge My righteous Servant shall justify many,

For He shall bear their iniquities.

¹²Therefore I will divide Him a portion with the great,

And He shall divide the spoil with the strong,

Because He poured out His soul unto death,

And He was numbered with the transgressors,

And He bore the sin of many,

And made intercession for the transgressors.

Many of these texts from Isaiah 53 are used by Handel in his *Messiah*. For example:

All we like sheep have gone astray;
We have turned, every one, to his own way.

That is a sad, sad statement, but notice how this is presented by Handel in a very lilting, very light manner, as sheep gamboling along over the hills, stupidly falling over cliffs, getting themselves entangled, falling into rivers and drowning. We have turned to our own way. "I did it my way," says the song, and say so many who ultimately drive their lives into a ditch—if not in this world, in that eternal ditch which yet remains in front of them when they die.

So Christ was the One who was oppressed and afflicted for us, "For the transgressions of My people He was stricken" (v. 8).

We read that "they made His grave with the wicked—But with the rich at His death" (v. 9).

We know from the New Testament that He was crucified between two thieves and placed in the grave of Joseph of Arimathea, a rich man. He was buried. The prophecy was fulfilled in every detail.

We read in verse 10 that "Yet it pleased the LORD to bruise Him; He has put Him to grief."

Why? Not that it was pleasant, but because "God so loved the world that He gave His only begotten Son" (John 3:16).

Why did He come? Isaiah tells us that He came to bear our sorrows. He came to be struck down by God and afflicted on our behalf. He was wounded and bruised because of our sins. We have all gone astray, but God the Father chose to use the horrible passion of His Son as the means of forgiveness (Isaiah 53:4-6). He came to offer a sacrifice.

The Jews in the Old Testament knew that the Messiah would be a great high priest to offer sacrifices, but they never dreamt He would offer Himself as a sacrifice. Today, when confronted with this prophecy from the Old Testament, a Jew will most likely say, "Well, that suffering Savior, that righteous one, is referring to the State of Israel." My friends, that just won't wash. Any investigation of this makes it very clear that this explanation will not do.

Even the greatest of the authorities of Jewish tradition and law, Maimonides, when this idea first appeared (in about 1100 A.D.), said that this is a false use of this prophecy. In other words, the great Jewish scholar said that Isaiah 53 referred to an individual messiah. He, who is regarded as the Jews' highest authority, said that this "individual" view is a view that had been held universally by Jews in all of the prior centuries. It is a picture of a suffering messiah who was to come to die for us. (Of course, tragically, Maimonides did not see Jesus as the Messiah.)

THE PASSION ACCORDING TO DAVID

Consider yet another passage from the ancient Hebrews pointing to Jesus Christ and His passion. Psalm 22 brings us right to the foot of the Cross. This was written by David, who came to the throne of Israel in 1010 B.C., and it provides a clear example of the inspiration of the Scriptures because of the fulfillment of these prophecies. Only an inspired Word would be able to prophesy all the things contained herein. Here are major portions of that psalm:

> ¹My God, My God, why have You forsaken Me?
> Why are You so far from helping Me,
> And from the words of My groaning? . . .

> ⁶But I am a worm, and no man;
> A reproach of men, and despised by the people.
> ⁷All those who see Me ridicule Me;
> They shoot out the lip, they shake the head, saying,
> ⁸"He trusted in the LORD, let Him rescue Him;
> Let Him deliver Him, since He delights in Him!". . .

1

¹¹Be not far from Me,

For trouble is near;

For there is none to help.

¹²Many bulls have surrounded Me;

Strong bulls of Bashan have encircled Me.

¹³They gape at Me with their mouths,

Like a raging and roaring lion.

¹⁴I am poured out like water,

And all My bones are out of joint;

My heart is like wax;

It has melted within Me.

¹⁵My strength is dried up like a potsherd,

And My tongue clings to My jaws;

You have brought Me to the dust of death.

¹⁶For dogs have surrounded Me;

The congregation of the wicked has enclosed Me.

They pierced My hands and My feet;

¹⁷I can count all My bones.

They look and stare at Me.

¹⁸They divide My garments among them,

And for My clothing they cast lots. . . .

²²I will declare Your name to My brethren;

In the midst of the assembly I will praise You. . . .

²⁷All the ends of the world

Shall remember and turn to the LORD,

And all the families of the nations

Shall worship before You.

²⁸For the kingdom is the LORD's,

And He rules over the nations.

³⁰A posterity shall serve Him.

will be recounted of the Lord to the next generation,
³¹They will come and declare His righteousness to a people who
will be born,
That He has done this.

There are contained here in Psalm 22 eight prophecies concerning Christ. Yet the possibility of only those eight being fulfilled has been estimated in the trillions—and again, these are just eight out of 333! Keep in mind that there are 325 other texts which also have been fulfilled. So only a book inspired by God could conceivably contain something like that.

One of the reasons God gave the Old Testament to the Hebrew people was that He might, through those prophecies, identify this One who was to come, so that when He did come He would be readily recognized as the true Messiah, and so Christ is.

Dr. Charles Augustus Briggs said that you could take this psalm and the accounts of the crucifixion of Christ in Matthew, Mark, Luke, and John and lay them side-by-side and see that they dovetail perfectly. In fact, there are more details on the crucifixion of Christ in this one psalm alone than there are in any single one of the Gospels. It is astonishing that someone could describe something more intimately and intricately a thousand years before it happened than it was recorded by those who witnessed it.

Let us look into this astonishing Messianic psalm, which begins with these familiar words: "My God, my God, why have You forsaken Me?" (v. 1). Immediately we are plunged into the depths of Christ's passion, the agony of His crucifixion, and toward the end of the three hours of darkness. Christ has, as it were, descended into the very blackness of Hell, and God has poured out His wrath upon Him after man had done his worst.

My God, My God, why have You forsaken Me?
Why are You so far from helping Me,

And from the words of My groaning? (v. 1).

This is a unique cry. Maybe you never realized this before, but Jesus rarely refers to God as "My God." He almost always refers to Him as "My Father."

- Even when Jesus was twelve years old He said, "Did you not know that I must be about My Father's business?" (Luke 2:49).
- When He taught us to pray He said,
    In this manner, therefore, pray:
    Our Father in heaven . . . (Matthew 6:9).
- When He gave His High Priestly Prayer, He said, "Father, the hour has come" (John 17:1).
- He began His words on the Cross with, "Father, forgive them, for they do not know what they do" (Luke 23:34).
- He ended those words on the Cross with "Father, into Your hands I commit My spirit" (Luke 23:46).

But there in the midst of the blackness of the infinite wrath of God, He diverts from all of His otherwise uniform experience and cries out, "My God, My God, why have You forsaken Me?" (Matthew 27:46).

Many theologians have struggled over that question, and it is a profound one. I think perhaps the most satisfying answer is that Christ is in such unbelievable agony and suffering so incredibly that which we may not know or cannot tell there in the depths of Hell. What would it mean to endure Hell? What would it be to endure Hell for a world of sinners? Jesus was finding out the absolute unbelievable agony of what the wrath of God would be like (thus causing Him to extrude blood through His pores the night before). So mind boggling, so staggering, so vast is His pain that it seems to Him that now God has forsaken Him and . . . He has.

I have heard liberal preachers say, "Jesus just *thought* God forsook Him; but, of course, He didn't." Wrong, my friend. That is what it is all about. Jesus was forsaken by God in order that we may *not* be forsaken by God. In the blinding, numbing agony, His human nature cries out, "Why have You forsaken Me?" Everyone had forsaken Him, as we shall see. He cries in the daytime and in the night season. The previous night He was in the garden crying out in agony for three hours. In the day season upon the Cross He has been crying out to God. "Our fathers trusted in You . . . and You delivered them." So it was with Abraham, Isaac, Jacob, and all of the rest. They trusted in God and God delivered them—but He did not deliver His own Son.

If you have ever been in great pain, you know how hard it is to think, let alone speak. Jesus was quoting this psalm to identify with it and to point the people to this Messianic passage at this very time—the time of its fulfillment.

"But I am a worm, and no man" (v. 6a). I think of some of the liberal revisionists of our hymnals. There is a familiar hymn that ends with the words, "Would He devote that sacred head/For such a worm as I?" You will probably not find it that way in many hymnals today because, you see, that is not good for our self-esteem. "I'm no worm," the revisionists say. Obviously, Jesus was considerably lower than we are, for He said,

> But I am a worm, and no man;
> A reproach of men, and despised by the people.
> All those who see Me ridicule Me;
> They shoot out the lip, they shake the head, saying,
> "He trusted in the LORD, let Him rescue Him;
> Let Him deliver Him, since He delights in Him!" (Psalm 22:6-8).

These very words were spoken by those who passed by—by the high priests, the elders, and the people.

Isn't it interesting that some people say Jesus conspired to fulfill all of the prophecies of the Old Testament. That would be quite a job. First thing you have to do is correctly choose your ancestors by multiple generations. Once you have mastered that, you work on getting the right parents. Then you have to make sure that you are born in the right place. When you figure out how to do those three things, get back to me, and I will tell you how to do the rest. There are only 330 other things you have to do.

I wonder how He got those who suffered with Him to mock Him. I wonder how He got the high priests to say these things? The very words the high priests used were recorded over a thousand years before that. In verse 12 we read, "Many bulls have surrounded Me; Strong bulls of Bashan have encircled Me."

He talks about the bulls and the dogs, the powerful ones and the vile ones, as these dogs that roamed in packs and killed people and ate those who were left on crosses overnight. Also, He talks about the sword, indicating the civil authorities, who all were turned against Him. Notice verse 13: "They gape at Me with their mouths, Like a raging and roaring lion."

Then He describes something of the agony He went through. By the way, David never went through anything vaguely approaching any of this.

> I am poured out like water,
> And all My bones are out of joint;
> My heart is like wax;
> It has melted within Me.
> My strength is dried up like a potsherd,
> And My tongue clings to My jaws; (vv. 14-15a).

So, we see that all of His bones are out of joint, an indication of the agonies of crucifixion, which tended to pull the bones out of joint in the body as a person hung upon a cross. We see an intimation of His cry, "I thirst," when He says "My tongue clings to My jaws," and "My strength is dried up like a potsherd." He goes on to say in verse 16: "For dogs have surrounded Me; The congregation of the wicked has enclosed Me."

This indicates that He was stationary and they were about Him. Then He says, "They pierced My hands and My feet" (v. 17). The average person reading that wouldn't perhaps grasp the full import of that statement. This was written in 1000 B.C. Crucifixion had not yet been invented. It was invented by the Phoenicians in 600 B.C., 400 years later. It was picked up several hundred years after that by the Romans. Yet, many centuries before all of that, David, by the Spirit of prophecy, says "They pierced My hands and My feet." David's hands and David's feet were never pierced. It goes on: "I can count all My bones. They look and stare at Me" (v. 17).

They stripped Him naked, and with His bones all pulled out of joint, He hangs in this shameful position of horror and agony before the crowd, many of whom were just sitting down and watching this horrendous spectacle.

And then we read, "They divide My garments among them, and for My clothing they cast lots" (v. 18).

A thousand years before the crucifixion, I wonder how Jesus managed to talk the Roman soldiers into doing that after they crucified Him? A little hard to explain, and yet it is amazing to me that one commentator today has had the unmitigated gall to say that Jesus arranged all of this to fulfill all of these prophecies and the 325 other prophecies. Then we read in this great culmination:

All the ends of the world
Shall remember and turn to the LORD,
And all the families of the nations
Shall worship before You.
For the kingdom is the LORD's,
And He rules over the nations (vv. 27-28).

When hundreds of millions of Christians attend church worldwide each week, we help fulfill that very prophecy. "All the ends of the world shall remember . . ." The Gospel of Jesus Christ is being spread into every nation—even in places where it is highly illegal. By the grace of God, one avenue of spreading the Gospel has been Evangelism Explosion, which I founded in the 1960s; and it has now penetrated into every nation on earth. They "shall remember and turn to the LORD, And all the families of the nations shall worship before You." What an incredible psalm this is.

CONSIDER THE ODDS

A mathematician, Peter Stoner, had his graduate students calculate what the odds would be of any one person fulfilling just eight of these prophecies. He found the chance was one in 10^{17}.[3] That is one in 100,000,000,000,000,000. Stoner gives an analogy to this. Suppose that we take 10^{17} silver dollars and lay them on the face of Texas. They will cover all of the state two feet deep. Mark one of these silver dollars and stir the whole mass thoroughly, all over the state. Blindfold a man and tell him that he can travel as far as he wishes, but he must pick up one silver dollar and say that this is the right one. What chance would he have of getting the right one? Just the same chance the prophets would have had of writing these eight prophecies and having them all come true in any one man, from their day to the present time. . . .[4]

If that isn't amazing enough, Stoner had his graduate students calculate the odds that any one person would fulfill 48 of these prophecies. The odds in that case were one in 10^{157}.[5] Again, we are talking about 333 prophecies fulfilled in Jesus.

Skeptic and journalist turned pastor, Lee Strobel, a former reporter at the *Chicago Tribune*, gives an analogy to the amazing predictions of Christ's suffering and crucifixion in Isaiah 53, written 700 years *before* the event: "That is like my trying to predict how the Cubs will do in the year 2693."[6]

So we see that the passion of Christ was foretold hundreds of years before He was even born. The Hebrew prophets told us of One who was born to die. Jesus of Nazareth fit the job description that was given to Him hundreds of years before His birth.

PART II

THE PASSION OF CHRIST

CHAPTER 3

THE WEEK THAT CHANGED THE WORLD

Then they brought the colt to Jesus and threw their clothes on it, and He sat on it. And many spread their clothes on the road, and others cut down leafy branches from the trees and spread them on the road.

MARK 11:7-8

JESUS OF NAZARETH, THE KING of kings and Lord of lords made His triumphal entry in humility. Just as He was born in a stable and laid in a food trough for animals—that is what a manger is—so He entered the city, not as an earthly king in a large chariot preceded by trumpeters. Instead, He came in humility, riding the foal of a donkey. This, too, fulfilled one of the Old Testament prophets. Zechariah said:

> Rejoice greatly, O daughter of Zion!
> Shout, O daughter of Jerusalem!
> Behold, your King is coming to you;
> He is just and having salvation,
> Lowly, and riding on a donkey,
> A colt, the foal of a donkey.
> —Zechariah 9:9

Jesus received glory from the humble masses, and yet from that time on we are told that the multitudes went back and followed Him no longer. Even the disciples in Gethsemane, when Christ was arrested, fled to save their own lives. Even those that shouted "Hosanna" on Sunday were on Friday morning screaming, "Crucify Him! Crucify Him!" Deserted, forsaken, abandoned, and rejected, Christ was all alone on a lonely Cross, on a lonely hill.

Two men were sitting on an airplane and getting acquainted. One was a businessman who worked for a large multi-national corporation that was doing operations in some 30 or 40 countries. When he asked the other one what he was involved in, he said he was involved in a family corporation that also had large extended operations. He said, "How many countries are you in?"

He said, "Well, actually, every one."

"Oho! really."

"You ah . . . work for Coca-Cola, right?"

"No. No."

"IBM?"

"No, much, much bigger than that."

"Oh, Microsoft."

"No, I'm afraid we have far more reps than they ever will."

He said, "I must say, I can't possibly imagine what that would be."

The man replied, "I am a minister of Jesus Christ."

What an astounding contrast. The largest organization that has ever existed on the face of the earth—two billion people as followers. Christianity has gone a long way from that lonely hill of Calvary, to say the least.

At the turn of the millennium, *Newsweek* ran a cover story about 2,000 years of Christianity. The author, Kenneth Woodward, wrote that though Christ was almost totally ignored during His lifetime, especially outside of the little enclave of Israel, 2,000 years later the centuries themselves are measured from the birth of Jesus of Nazareth. Our calendars—not only in America and Europe, but in the Middle East and in India and China, all over—refer to the birth of Jesus Christ.

A third of the world's population claims to be His followers—two billion people. Woodward goes on to say:

> By any secular standard, Jesus is also the dominant figure of Western culture. Like the millennium itself, much of what we now think of as Western ideas, inventions, and values finds its source or inspiration in the religion that worships God in his name. Art and science, the self and society, politics and economics, marriage and the family, right and wrong, body and soul—all have been touched and often radically transformed by Christian influence.[7]

Emperors and governors were the men in power back then—kings and rulers—but now their bodies rot in their graves and their souls await the final judgment. They have no followers today. No one worships them; no one serves them or awaits their bidding. But it is not so with Jesus, said Napoleon Bonaparte, who was well acquainted with political power. In fact, it is impossible or unimaginable that anyone would wait on the bidding of some Roman Caesar moldering in his grave, and yet hundreds of millions of people all over the world wait on the bidding of Jesus Christ and seek, above all else in this life, to do His will.

The original Holy Week—beginning with Palm Sunday and culminating with Easter—is the week that changed the world. The most thoroughly reported week in history was covered by four reporters, who were either eyewitnesses themselves or who drew on eyewitness material. We know more about these eight days, from Sunday to Sunday, than any other eight days in the ancient historical period in our world. From these we get a very detailed account of everything that went on at that time.

Most people are known for what they did in their lives. We have Alexander Graham Bell and the telephone, Edison and the light bulb, Ford and the car, but, as we saw in the first chapter, Christ is known most of all for the fact that He died. It is the Cross of Christ, the instrument on which He died that is remembered and that is lifted up above almost every church in the world. He accomplished by His death more than all other men combined have accomplished by their lives.

He was a wanted man. He had a price on His head. The authorities were seeking Him. Search parties had gone out all over seeking this One to bring Him to the authorities. Where was He hiding? Right at the head of a large and tumultuous parade that was walking and singing and shouting and coming right into the gates of Jerusalem. What audacity. It took raw courage to walk right into the mouth of the lion—those that were waiting to take Him and kill Him.

Even the soldiers that Caiaphas sent came back empty-handed. He asked them, "Why have you not brought Him?" They said, "No man ever spoke like this Man!" (John 7:46), and there He was walking right into the city. More than that, He was walking up the steps of the temple. We read that He walked all around and looked upon all things and gave them ample opportunity. Finally, when sundown came, He turned, walked out and went back to Bethany.

That was Sunday when He rode into the city riding upon a colt. It is amazing how many little things we pass over in the Scripture without noticing them, but everything in the Bible is of tremendous import. He came, according to the prophecy, riding upon a colt, a young donkey. We read that Jesus told two of His disciples, "Go into the village opposite you . . . you will find a colt tied, . . . Loose it and bring it here. And if anyone says to you, 'Why are you doing this?' say, 'The Lord has need of it,' and immediately he will send it here" (Mark 11:2-3). And so they brought this colt, and Jesus mounted the colt and sat on it.

Nothing remarkable about this passage, is there? You missed it, didn't you? The colt was one, we are told, "on which no one has sat." You don't get on the colt of a donkey that no man ever sat upon or broke unless you are interested in getting tossed about ten feet up in the air and landing on your head. But Jesus is the sovereign Lord of everything. He is the Lord of the winds, and He is Lord of the sea and the waves. He is Lord of the trees that wither at His curse. He is Lord of the fishes who bring up tax money at His command. He is Lord of everything. He is Lord of the animal kingdom as well—as this colt could attest. Later, a rooster would give evidence, when it crowed at just the time that Jesus said that it would.

So, here He is, the Lord of glory, and the Sadducees and Pharisees come running out, and when the people shout, "Blessed is the King who comes in the name of the LORD" (Luke 19:38), they called out to Him, "Teacher, rebuke Your disciples" (Luke 19:39b). In other words, "Teacher, tell your disciples to keep silent." Jesus said, ". . . if these should keep silent, the stones would immediately cry out" (Luke 19:40b) No, there is no way that silence could be held at that time, for the Son of God had come to His own.

That was the first day of the week. On the next day, Jesus came in and cleansed the temple, as He had done at the beginning of His ministry (John 2:13-17). If they weren't angry enough with Him earlier, they were really furious now.

We read that He sought solitude on Wednesday. He separated Himself, and He was alone. It was the calm before the storm. Jesus was no doubt engaged in prayer, asking God for strength for the great ordeal that awaited Him. You will recall that Wednesday night He was at Bethany, where Mary anointed His feet with precious ointment and prepared Him for His burial. One disciple was particularly angry at the supposed waste, and that was Judas.

Finally, on that Wednesday night, Jesus retired to His borrowed room in the house of Lazarus, and laid Himself down to sleep for the last time in His life. When He awoke the next morning, He awoke to never sleep again. It was Thursday, a day of action, a day when many things were beginning to take place. The priests' scheme to take Him fell into place when Judas came and offered to betray Him.

That night Jesus and the disciples had the Passover together. The disciples were arguing among themselves about which one should be greatest in the kingdom of God, and Jesus answered them by taking off His robe, girding Himself with a towel and basin, and washing their feet. "If anyone desires to be first, he shall be last of all and servant of all" (Mark 9:35).

Later, Thursday night they went into the Garden of Gethsemane. Jesus takes His three innermost disciples, Peter, James, and John and goes farther, and then leaves them to watch and pray. He goes yet farther Himself and throws Himself down and begins to pray. He prays: "O My Father . . . let this cup pass from me" (Matthew 26:39). He comes back an hour later and the disciples are asleep, and He says, "What! Could you not watch with Me one hour?" (Matthew 26:40). "Again, a second time, He went away and prayed, saying, O My Father, if this cup cannot pass away from Me unless I drink it, Your will be done" (Matthew 26:42).

He goes back just as Judas and the soldiers and the servants of the high priest arrive, and He steps forward and says, "Whom are you seeking?" (John 18:4b); and they said, "Jesus of Nazareth." He said, "I am He." At least that is what the English text says, but in the Greek text it simply says, "I am," which in the Old Testament is the great name of Jehovah, "I AM THAT I AM" (Exodus 3:14). He exudes from Himself such power that all of them go backward and fall onto the ground. This was just a little touch of the power they really were dealing with. If He had wished to, He could have swept them all into Hell with simply the blink of His eye.

No, Jesus was no martyr to a cause. He came as a willing sacrifice to give Himself for our sins, and so the disciples all forsake Him and flee. He undergoes six mock trials before being put to death for our sins.

How fickle is public opinion! On Palm Sunday, the crowds loudly cheered His triumphant entry into Jerusalem. Five days later, the crowds clamored for His execution. I repeat, how fickle public opinion is. How fickle is the fame and applause of men, and yet many people spend their whole lives seeking it.

This is the greatest Person that has ever lived. He is the King of the Ages that has turned the river of the centuries out of its course. Christ is marching on. His kingdom gathers greater force and greater power with every passing year and is accelerating as never before. In the last twenty years there have been more people brought into the kingdom of God than in the entire rest of the history of the world. Are you part of the greatest movement on this planet? Everything else that thinks itself so important is nothing, nothing but the backdrop, the scenery in the greatest drama of the ages, the drama of the Son of God going forth conquering and to conquer by His love the hearts and minds and wills of men and women. Everything else is dross. Are you part of His Kingdom work?

What do people spend their lives doing? Seeking for fame? Fortune? The things of this world? Houses and lands and cars and all of these things? When Jesus dragged His Cross down the Via Dolorosa, that way of sorrows, He took something else with Him. Did you ever think what it was? What was it that Jesus, in addition to that heavy Cross, was taking with Him? He was taking with Him every last single thing He owned, and that very shortly would be removed . . . His clothing. Nothing else. Everything else He borrowed. There is a poem that captures it well.

> They borrowed a bed to lay His head
>   When Christ the Lord came down;
> They borrowed the ass in the mountain pass
>   For Him to ride to town:
> But the Crown that He wore and the Cross
>   that He bore
> Were His own—
>   The Cross was His own.
> He borrowed the dish of broken fish
>   With which He satisfied; . . .
> They borrowed the bread when the crowd
>   He fed
> On the grassy mountain side;

But the crown that He wore and the Cross
    that He bore
Were His own—
    The Cross was His own.
He borrowed the ship in which to sit
To teach the multitude;
He borrowed the next in which to rest,
He had never a home so rude; . . . .
They borrowed a room on the way to the tomb,
The Passover lamb to eat.
They borrowed a cave, for Him a grave,
They borrowed a winding sheet.
But the crown that He wore
    And the Cross that He bore
Were His own.
    (Author unknown)

That Cross was His own. I learned that poem about fifty years ago, and I have always been touched by it. But there is one thing I discovered—one fault it has: It's not true, is it? That Cross was not His own. It was mine and it was yours, but it wasn't His. We deserve the nails in our hands and feet, and we deserve that crown of thorns upon our head. No, that Cross belonged to you and me.

Also belonging to us were the dreaded and foul contents of the bitter cup that the Son of God drank on our behalf. He was beginning to endure for our sakes the sufferings we deserve because of our sins. His passion was just beginning.

CHAPTER *4*

CHRIST'S BITTER CUP

O My Father, if it is possible, let this cup pass from Me;
nevertheless, not as I will, but as You will.

MATTHEW 26:39

THE PALM BRANCHES ARE waving in the bright sunshine. The people shout joyfully. Praises echo off the Judean hills: "Hosanna to the Son of David!" "Blessed is He that comes in the name of the Lord!" "The King of Glory is coming to Jerusalem!"

Suddenly, the scene changes. The wind blows and all is different. The bright sunlight gives way to deep darkness. The multitude has disappeared. The palm branches are replaced by the eerie shadowy branches of the ancient gnarled olive trees. The excited tumult is silenced. There is no sound but the soft moaning of the breeze through the leaves. Jesus has come to the garden of the oil press: The Garden of Gethsemane.

As we follow Him deeper into Holy Week, and as we come to the very gate of the Garden of Gethsemane, a certain unnamed awe grips our souls and causes us to draw back. Here we enter upon holy ground. Our Lord is over-burdened, He is borne down to the ground, and He is in indescribable agony. It seems that we should not be here at all, that it is almost a desecration to pull back the veil and to gaze upon this ghastly scene that is taking place before our eyes.

CHRIST'S PRAYER

For there is Christ, flat upon His face, in great agony of spirit. His heart is sorrowful, so that He is wrung out with an anguish beyond comprehension. Blood oozes out of His pores. In agony of soul, Christ cries out to His Father, "O My Father, if it is possible, let this cup pass from Me" (Matthew 26:39). Immediately we start back. We are appalled. We should not even have been here to look upon this scene or to listen to these words. Can this be the mighty Son of God who stretched forth His hands and stilled the sea and calmed the winds and who now cries out in anguish?

Skeptics down through the centuries have been quick to clutch at these words, like some vulture clutching at a prey, and to use them to ridicule and mock Christ. Celsus, the first great antagonist who wrote against Christ in the second century—Celsus, that vain pagan philosopher, says with scorn: "Why then does He supplicate help and bewail Himself and pray for escape from the fear of death? If He is who the Christians say He is, what does He here on His face lamenting so?"

Or Julian, the Apostate, that emperor of Rome, who attempted to destroy Christianity and reestablish the pagan religions of Rome, dips his pen in sarcasm and writes the following words: "Jesus presents such petitions as a wretched mortal would offer when, unable to bear a calamity with serenity, . . ." This was no picture of a Roman stoic, able to bear whatever came to him with equanimity. No, indeed. This was something far different.

Multitudes of unbelievers have used this occasion to make a comparison—a most disparaging comparison—between Christ and Socrates. They compare this wretched scene of the Galilean on His face in agony with the "heroic" Socrates, taking the cup of hemlock and calmly and serenely drinking it down and lying down to die without complaint, without petition, without prayer—simply "dying as a man should die."

What should we say then? Is Christ to be so disparagingly compared to Socrates? Is our Savior less than the Athenian philosopher? Absolutely not.

If Christ were merely a great teacher, as some have erroneously declared, surely His teaching founders upon the rocks of Gethsemane.

If He were merely a great example, as some have set forth, surely His example is crushed in the oil press of Gethsemane. If Jesus were merely a preacher and nothing more, certainly all of the glory of Christ is destroyed here in the grave of Gethsemane. But we know that Jesus is much more than a great teacher, more than a great example, more than a preacher. Rather, He is the one Mediator between God and man. He came to take away sin. He came to destroy the works of the devil. He is ". . . the Lamb of God who takes away the sin of the world" (John 1:29b).

All of us who have ever felt the sting and pang of guilt in our own should know the meaning of Christ's prayer in the Garden. We who have transgressed the holy law of a holy God, who have felt the batteries of Sinai being lowered upon our souls, who have heard the thunderous roar of the artillery of God's law aimed at us, know the meaning of that prayer.

SIN OF THE WORLD

What was in that mysterious cup which appeared before Christ's face there in the darkness of Gethsemane? In that cup was *sin—all of the sin of the world.*

Imagine with me, if you will, visiting the Centers for Disease Control in Atlanta. You go into a large sealed room and see hundreds of beakers which you are told contain the distillation of the germs, the bacteria, and the viruses for all of the most dangerous diseases known to mankind. Think of them all: The black plague, AIDS, syphilis, gonorrhea, small pox, and every foul disease man has ever known. There you see a technician unstop vial after vial and pour the cultures of each one into a large beaker with the accumulation of all of the deadly diseases facing humankind.

Would it not be our tendency to shrink back farther and farther away from that horror, that beaker of death that now stands before us? If you were asked to touch it, you would recoil with terror. Should you be told that you must drink its contents, the most unimaginable dread and fear would fill your soul, but that is as nothing compared to what Jesus saw that dark night in Gethsemane.

I once saw a film in which a man suddenly, precipitously, stepped inside a small hut, not knowing who or what was inside. There in a dimly lit room, he found himself standing face to face with a man whose features were horribly distorted by what he immediately recognized as the dread disease of leprosy. Instantly, his soul shrank back, and the desire to flee, to run as far and as fast as he could, almost overwhelmed him. Would not we, each one, do the same?

But can you imagine being trapped in a small room with a dozen or more lepers all around you, reaching out and touching you, handling your hands, breathing in your face? Would you not recoil with the utmost horror? No, you would not—if you were a leper, but for one who is not a leper, it would be more horrible than we could possibly describe.

We do not recoil from the horror of sin because *we* are the sinners; we are in the midst of sin daily. It is touching us. We handle it daily. We participate in it—sometimes joyfully. It is part of our lives.

Ah, but for Jesus, the undefiled One, the Pure One, that Paragon of Virtue, for Him what horror and dread filled His soul as He looked in that cup filled with sin.

However, there was more than sin in that cup. Jesus had often said, (in effect) "You all shall go away and forsake me and leave me alone. But I am not alone, for my Father is with me." How He delighted to say, "Father I know that You always hear Me" (John 11:41-42). Always He dwelt in that intimate communion of the presence of His Father's love, but now *He looked into that cup and saw in there all the sins of the world*:

- All of the sin since Cain first smashed the brains of his brother Abel,
- All the sins of Auschwitz and the Gulag Archipelago,
- All of the vile sins of blasphemy and profanity,

- All of the vile sins of fornication and adultery and sodomy and lesbianism,
- All of the sins of the flesh,
- All of the anger and hatred,
- All of the jealousy and the lust . . .

. . . all were squeezed and distilled in that singular cup.

ABANDONMENT BY GOD

As bad as that was, there was more than the sin of the world in that cup. There was also to be found in that bitter cup *the dreaded abandonment by God*—by that One who is of purer eyes than even to look upon iniquity. As noted earlier, Jesus was abandoned by God. For though He merely looked into the cup that night, in the noontime darkness the following day, that cup was once more extended before His face by an arm that reached down from the everlasting hills, even the arm of His Father. Jesus would take that vial—that noxious liquid, and drink it down. Christ, who knew no sin, became sin for us. ". . . the LORD has laid on Him the iniquity of us all" (Isaiah 53:6b). God has made Him to be sin for us (2 Corinthians 5:21).

He felt that the worm was in the very marrow of His bones. That sin was in His very body and soul. Jesus Christ, the pure spotless Son of God, became the greatest sinner who ever lived. All of the guilt of the world was piled upon Him. Christ became the arch-criminal of the universe. God looked down upon His beloved Son and saw sin and turned His back on Him. Jesus was abandoned by His Father.

"My God, My God, why have You forsaken Me?" (Matthew 27:46b). Ah, look within thyself and see the guilt of man's iniquity, and the answer to that is clear. He was forsaken by God and abandoned by His Father. There He hung, quivering with all of the loathsomeness and vileness of sin—alone and abandoned by God.

CURSE OF THE INVIOLABLE LAW

There is yet a third ingredient in that cup. Beyond the sin of the world and the abandonment of God, there is also *the dreadful curse of the inviolable law of God*. Christ now becomes the cosmic criminal. All of the batteries of God's holy law are lowered upon Him. God whets His arrow, bends the bow, and sinks into Christ's soul the arrow of His wrath. Jesus Christ feels the anger of God against sin as God takes, as it were, the great cauldron of the fiery wrath of His anger for sin and pours it out upon His beloved Son. That lava flowing into the very veins of the Son of God is consuming and extinguishing sin. Oh, the exquisite and excruciating pain—the curse of God. Well it has been said:

> We may not know, we cannot tell
> What pains He had to bear,
> But we believe it was for us
> He hung and suffered there.[8]

Christ endured in His own body and soul such agony, such suffering, as no mortal, finite man could ever begin to comprehend. What does it mean to suffer Hell? What would it mean to suffer Hell for *every* man?

DEMONIC ATTACK

Even more than these, there was a fourth element in that cup—a final, fatal, deadly element: Rejected by men and abandoned by God, *Jesus Christ is now given over to demons*. He feels the ground falling away beneath His feet. A great chasm opens up in the earth and Christ plummets into the very bottomless pit of Hell, there to be met by a cacophony of cackling demons that fall upon Him with fangs and claw.

It is always an interesting phenomenon to see a judge fall afoul of the law and be himself sentenced to prison, where he must then live and mingle with scores or even hundreds of men whom he had condemned to precede him there. These demons, these archfiends, which had been condemned by Christ in Heaven, who had been cast out of Paradise into the pit of Hell, now fall upon their judge.

The only claim Satan has upon any of us is due to our sins. It was by sin that we were sold into slavery and captivity to Satan, but no such sin existed in the life of Christ, who would say, ". . . for the ruler of this world is coming, and he has nothing in Me" (John 14:30b). Now he has everything in Christ. All of the sin of the world is upon Him; He is given over into the hands of demons. That was the hour and power of darkness.

When that roaring lion leaped upon Samson, he tore its jaws apart and killed it with his mighty arms. When One who is "greater than Samson" finds Himself with a roaring lion, Satan—that great lion out of the pit leaps upon Him with fang and claw. But Christ is secured to a tree and can do nothing to defend Himself. He came to Calvary for this very purpose—to endure the penalty for sin in our place.

All of this was in that bitter cup. Jesus said, "O My Father, if it is possible, let this cup pass from Me." It was not possible if there was to be any hope for us.

Socrates and Christ? Socrates, indeed. Dare any man make such an invidious comparison between Socrates and Christ? Socrates—

- that flat-nosed son of a midwife;
- that vain philosopher;
- that one who, not satisfied with Xanthippe, his wife, had two sons by a concubine;
- who stooped to usury;
- who pleaded with the court to save his life;
- who was willing to give money to be spared;
- who took the cup from a weeping jailer, drank it and lay comfortably down in the midst of adoring disciples and slowly went to sleep.

Is this man to be compared with the heroic young Son of God who, in the midst of His life—

- was betrayed by a friend,
- was forsaken by His disciples,
- was mocked by the religious leaders of the day,
- was condemned by the authorities,
- was abandoned by God,
- was given over to demons,
- who drank down the cup of sin and suffered the infinite wrath of God?

Socrates, indeed. There is no room for any comparison at all. There is between Socrates and Christ the distance of infinity.

Christ's bitter cup. I would have you to know that it wasn't Christ's cup at all—it was ours. The sin was ours, the abandonment should have been ours, the demons should have been ours, and the curse should have been ours—but Christ took it for us.

How can we ever thank Him enough? Christ has consumed that bitter cup and transformed it into a cup of blessing for us—as in the cup of the Lord's Table.

A PERMANENT MEMORIAL

To make sure we don't forget Him and the incredible price of the passion, Jesus instituted the Lord's Table, where we consume the elements in a permanent memorial. He said, "Do this in remembrance of Me" (Luke 22:19). It is interesting, I believe, that He does not tell us to do it in remembrance of His doctrine or in remembrance of His teaching. Christianity is not based upon the teachings of Christ, the teachings of its Founder; it is not based upon the doctrines of its Founder. It is based upon *Him*. "Do this in remembrance of *Me*," upon His person, upon His birth, His life, His death, His resurrection. This is the basis for the Christian faith.

This is not to say that His teaching and His doctrine are not important, but they are not the foundation of our hope of everlasting life.

Remember Him in His temptation.

Remember Him in His vilification, as He was falsely judged and charged with all sorts of evils. He was called a winebibber and a glutton. He was called Beelzebub, the prince of demons. He was called an imposter and a fraud.

Remember Him in His crucifixion, where He was enduring the penalty of death that we deserve—when His hands and feet were pierced, His body was broken, His blood was shed.

Remember Him in His abandonment, as God the Father abandoned His beloved Son.

Remember Him as He took our guilt and endured the wrath of God in our place.

Remember Him.

The great Medieval monk, Saint Bernard of Clairvaux, wrote the hymn, "Jesus the very thought of Thee." One of the lines in that hymn states, "The love of Jesus, what it is, none but His loved ones know."⁹

CHAPTER 5

VIA DOLOROSA

And when they had mocked Him, they took the
robe off Him, put His own clothes on Him, and led Him
away to be crucified.

MATTHEW 27:31

CHRIST IS THE TOUCHSTONE OF character. What we really are in the depths of our souls is revealed by our encounter with Him. I remember a lovely lady who often waited upon my wife and me when we visited a certain store. She was a pure delight. She was lovely of face and figure and had a marvelous personality. She was exceedingly gracious and yet dignified and friendly and warm. One day my wife, while visiting the store, entered into a conversation with the lady, and she brought up the subject of Christ and her relationship to him.

My wife, in relating the incident to me, said, "The strangest thing happened. This woman seemed to be transfigured before my eyes, and her countenance was changed. She became glaringly opposed to all that I was saying." Her true nature was revealed. Christ is the touchstone of the real character of our soul.

CHARACTERS IN THE DRAMA

In the final scene in the great drama of the life and death of Jesus Christ, many come into contact with Christ and have their deepest selves revealed. They appear ostensibly to judge and condemn Christ. But, in actuality, they come to be irradiated by the brilliant light that emanates from the Son of God and to have revealed the depths of their own soul—the real nature of their own character—that they, indeed, might be tried and judged, condemned or acquitted.

Here we see the Pharisees, who hounded the steps of Jesus throughout His ministry. Here are the Sadducees, as well as the high priests and the Sanhedrin. Here we find Pilate, the Roman governor; and Herod, that dilapidated and dissipated king of Galilee. Here we find Peter, the denier; Judas the apostate; Annas, that wily old ecclesiastical politician; and Caiaphas, who conceived the whole horrid plot in his own depraved mind. They are all here for one final reprise on the stage of history in the drama of the ages on the Via Dolorosa—the dolorous way, the way of sorrows, the way of suffering, the way of grief, the way of pain.

Most specifically, the Via Dolorosa stretched from the praetorian of Pilate to the hill of Golgotha. But in a larger sense, that dolorous way began when Christ left the ivory palaces of Paradise and stepped down into the stench of a filthy stable to be born of a woman, to be born under the law, to be born as our substitute. For Jesus, all of that way was a "Via Dolorosa." He was, indeed, "a man of sorrows and acquainted with grief." He came to suffer that we might rejoice.

Some of the characters in the passion also include:

- Barabbas, a prisoner in for murder, who was released by Pilate as a good-will gesture—only one gets the impression that Pilate would have preferred for the people to choose Jesus over the murderer.
- Longinus, the Roman centurion who crucified the Savior. It was he who uttered the famous words, "Truly this Man was the Son of God" (Mark 15:39b).
- The Apostle Thomas, who was not present when Jesus first appeared to the apostles risen from the dead. His story is part of the "many infallible proofs" by which Jesus showed His disciples He was risen from the dead (Acts 1:3).

A GREAT INJUSTICE

What happened to Jesus on that Thursday night and Friday during the day overflows with judicial errors and crimes. First of all, the judge and the jury should not be seeking witnesses at all, much less just witnesses *against* Him. In fact, Jewish law required that the people go to great lengths to seek witnesses to defend the defendant. Furthermore, they certainly should not have been seeking false witnesses and paying them, suborning them to witness falsely. They should not have been seeking witnesses to testify against Him to put Him to death. The end had already been determined before the prisoner was ever captured. These are just a few of the forty-eight violations of law that are seen in this kangaroo court.

I think that as an aside, it is interesting that the UPI reported that an Israeli lawyer by the name of Itzhak David, an Orthodox Jew, appealed to the high court of Israel to have Jesus Christ exonerated and all charges against Him dropped. He wanted it declared that this was, indeed, a mistrial filled with violations of Jewish law. The Supreme Court heard this request for a *writ of certiorari*, and they denied it.

As they hurled accusation after accusation against Jesus at these mock trials, a fascinating point comes out about truth versus lies. Are they not interesting—these witnesses *against* Christ? They came from all parts of the city, contradicting each other, lying, willing to perjure themselves—false witnesses, not able to agree with one another, nor even with themselves. Then notice the later witnesses that we see *for* Christ—holy men—the disciples and beyond—men who consistently agreed in their testimony—men who sealed that testimony with their own blood. There were martyrs and saints of God—men and women who were fed to lions, burned alive, and boiled in oil.

The devil is a prince of lies and has been from the beginning. How many people has he told with his malicious whispers, "The evidence for the Bible contradicts itself"? Why does he whisper that so often, so continually, and so loudly?

For decades I have handed my Bible to innumerable people who have made that charge and said, "That's wonderful. I have been reading the Bible for years and I have never noticed it myself. Would you please show me where it contradicts itself?" I am still waiting to be shown. But ignorant people who, in many cases, have never even read the Bible through, will very boldly asseverate that the Bible contradicts itself in many places. They declare that the evidences for Christ and the witnesses for Christ contradict one another. The truth is, as Satan well knows, that it is the witnesses *against* Christ who contradict themselves.

As the witnesses accused Jesus, what was His response?

Jesus was silent. Silently He had stood there, but now He was going to speak. Caiaphas would not have spoken had he been in that position, but Jesus did, and the whole world waited. I have heard people say, "Jesus never claimed to be the Messiah—it is some claim that we have made for Him." Here He is, before the supreme court of the Jews, charged by the high priest and put under oath. "I adjure You by the living God that You tell us if You are the Christ, the Son of God" (Matthew 26:63).

The Christ—the Messiah—opened His lips. Angels bent low; generations of people yet unborn are waiting to hear. Will there be a firm foundation placed beneath our faith? Is this, indeed, the One that should come, or do we look for another? "It is as you said. . . . I am."

With that the priest took the neck of his robe and tore it apart and said, "He has spoken blasphemy . . . you have heard His blasphemy. What do you think?" They answered and said, "He is deserving of death" (Matthew 26:65-66).

I ask you: Is that true? Why was Jesus silent? Is it not often the case that a person is silent because he is giving tacit consent? Could that be the case? Many accusations were made against Him, and yet He denied none of them. Was he perchance guilty? In the answer to that lies the very heart of the Christian faith, and we must uncompromisingly declare that Jesus Christ was silent precisely because He *was guilty*. He was guilty of everything with which He was charged, and He was guilty of many crimes for which He was not charged. He was guiltier than any man who had ever stood before the Sanhedrin. He was guiltier than the vilest miscreant who shall ever stand before the judgment bar of God. He was the guiltiest man who ever lived . . . but the guilt He bore was not His own. It was yours and it was mine. "The LORD has laid on Him the iniquity of us all" (Isaiah 53:6b).

God made Him to be sin for us. Guilty—as charged.

Did the Jews crucify Christ? There has been much controversy surrounding Mel Gibson's movie, *The Passion of The Christ.* Based on some of the charges made, one would think this film would reopen old wounds in Judeo-Christian relations, that this film would cause some new pogrom. There is no question that inexcusable atrocities have been perpetuated against the Jews through the ages by so-called "Christians," who have used the death of Christ as an excuse for venting their anti-Semitism.

But such a pogrom has *never* happened in countries where evangelicalism has played a major role. Rabbi Daniel Lapin, an Orthodox Jew who appreciates Jesus and Christians, has pointed out on our television program that modern America is not the same as medieval Europe. He points out that the United States of America has given Jews something no other country has ever given them: "No country in the last two thousand years has provided the same haven of tranquility and prosperity for Jews as has the United States of America. This is not in spite of Americans being Christian; it is *because* of it. You might say that America's Bible belt is the Jewish community's safety belt."[10]

So I raise the question again—did the Jews crucify Christ? There can be no question of the fact that the plot was conceived by Caiaphas, the high priest. It was carried out by the Sanhedrin, with the help of Judas, but that is not all of the answer. The Romans were involved and actually performed, as Gentiles, the actual crucifixion, so we may say that it was the Jews and the Romans. However, if we do that, we still will have missed the point—for is it not of a truth that it was all of us who were involved in His death? It was because of our sins that He died. Yet, if we see it merely as that, we still fail to see the truth, because it was really neither Jews nor Gentiles nor Romans nor all of us who crucified Christ, for He boldly declared, "I lay down my life that I might take it again. No one takes it from Me, but I lay it down of Myself. I have power to lay it down, and I have power to take it again" (John 10:17-18).

So who killed Christ?

It was Mother Teresa who placed that thorny crown upon His head.

It was Billy Graham who hammered in those nails.

It was Francis Schaeffer who placed the occupied Cross in its place on Calvary.

It was you.

It was I.

RELIGIOUS BUT LOST

Caiaphas typifies the vast multitude of people who have since lived and can be described by these three words: *religious but lost.* He held the highest position that could be held in the religion of his people, and yet he was as blind and lost as any man ever was. How vast is the multitude that suppose that because they are a member of some church, have received its sacraments, hold some office, (deacon, elder, trustee, president of the women's group, teacher of a Sunday school) that all is well with their souls. One day they will hear the words of Christ, the great final Judge, who will say, "Depart from Me. I never knew you."

As we will see in a later chapter, Caiaphas operated on a philosophy of expediency versus obedience. The interesting thing about expediency is that in the long run, it never works. Frequently, over the short haul, it will. "Lest the Romans come and take away our place and our nation"—this expedient action must be taken. Note well: the Romans came in 36 A.D. Vitellius, king of Syria, the Roman governor, came and deposed Joseph Caiaphas for misdeeds in office. Fact two: the Romans came in 70 A.D. and took away their nation and crucified over 100,000

Jews, destroying thousands more, and led the rest into captivity. Expediency is usually a poor expedient.

FURTHER DOWN THE VIA DOLOROSA

As we continue to travel with Him along that doleful road, we find Him, at length, coming to stand before Pontius Pilate, the governor, the procurator of Judea. In the overall worldwide scheme of things, Pontius Pilate was a very inconsiderable person—a procurator of a small part of an insignificant kingdom at the eastern end of the gigantic Roman Empire.

He would never have been heard of at all were it not for the simple fact that one day he stood in the presence of Jesus Christ. Because of that brief encounter, he shall be remembered when all of the rest of Rome has been forgotten. When the greatest Roman of them all, Julius Caesar, has fallen into oblivion, when the Coliseum itself has completely disintegrated into dust, the name of Pontius Pilate will still be known to the civilized world. "Born of the Virgin Mary, suffered under Pontius Pilate . . .," as the Apostle's Creed declares. What a terrible epitaph for anyone.

Pontius Pilate. Pontius was his family name, from the Latin *pons*, which means "a bridge," and Pilate from the Latin *pilatus*, meaning "one who handles a spear." So he was standing that day as never before upon a bridge, which, unbeknownst to him, was anchored on one side to Heaven and on the other side to Hell. With his spear, that symbol of Roman authority and power, he could have held at bay the high priests and the Sanhedrin, who were thirsting for the blood of Jesus. He could have upheld the justice of Rome. But, rather, because he was at heart a weak man, a selfish man, a little man, he caved in; and Pilate turned and whirled and threw that spear right into the heart of Jesus Christ.

It was a subordinate of his, the centurion, who actually handled the spear. But in a very real way, it was Pilate whose authority was behind the deed. By acquiescing to the sinful desires of others who were hungering after Jesus' death, he has forever brought shame upon the name of Pontius Pilate.

Pilate asked Jesus, "What is truth?" He then turned around and left, not waiting to hear His answer, thereby showing himself to be a moral relativist. Pilate would feel very much at home in our day, for we live in a nation full of Pontius Pilates—these agnostics as to the truth. Oh, they put it slightly differently. They will say something like, "Well, all truth is relative." In fact, the one single thing that almost every student in America coming out of public schools agrees on when entering college is that all truth is relative.[11] Of that they are certain. If you ask them how they know that, they will probably say, "Have you never heard of the theory of relativity? All truth is therefore relative. Einstein said so" . . . and they feel very educated. No, he didn't. What Einstein said is that relativity applies to the realm of *physics*—not *ethics*.

Paul Johnson, the great historian and author of the blockbuster book, *Modern Times*, points out: "Mistakenly, but perhaps inevitably, relativity became confused with relativism. No one was more distressed than Einstein by this public misapprehension. . . . Einstein was not a practicing Jew, but he acknowledged a God. He believed passionately in absolute standards of right and wrong."[12]

When a person says there are no absolutes, what they are really saying (and what every professor and every teacher in every public school who says there are no absolutes, is saying in a cowardly fashion) is, "I am an atheist."

My friends, God is the ultimate absolute. He is the absolute God, the omnipotent, omniscient, all-present God, the absolute One. So, anyone who says there are no absolutes, is saying there is no God. They are also saying that God has not spoken, and we have no word from Him, for any word from the absolute God is, by definition, an absolute truth. God could not possibly lie.

Today our nation is filled with agnostics and atheists who say, "What is truth? There is no real truth." You probably have heard them say something like this, for example, in response to the Gospel: "Well, that may be true for you, but it's not true for me"—which is simply another way of saying there are no absolutes.

If the truth of God is absolute, then it is absolutely true for everybody in the world. When God's Word declares, "for all have sinned and fall short of the glory of God" (Romans 3:23), that is a fact and it applies to absolutely every single person on this planet. God's truth is absolute because God is the ultimate absolute in the universe.

But Pilate was an agnostic as far as truth is concerned. The word *agnostic* means "one who doesn't know." Agnostic comes from two Greek words (gnosis, the word for "knowledge," and the alpha privative "a," which means the same as "un") meaning lack of knowledge, no knowledge, no truth, we don't know, we're ignorant of this matter. The Apostle Paul said, "For I do not desire, brethren, that you should be ignorant . . ." (Romans 11:25a).

Interestingly, the word agnostic and the word ignorant have the same meaning. While the word agnostic comes from Greek, the word ignorant comes from Latin. They mean exactly the same: no knowledge, without knowledge. So when someone says to you, "Oh, I'm an agnostic," you might simply say to them, "Well, I'm sorry to hear you are ignorant."

The Apostle Paul said, "Moreover, brethren, I would not that ye should be ignorant" (1 Corinthians 10:1 KJV). The Greek word here is agnostic. "I would not have you to be agnostic," because the Bible says we may know: "These things I have written to you . . . that you may know that you have eternal life" (1 John 5:13)—that you may *know* that the Word of God is truth, absolute truth.

JESUS—INCARNATE TRUTH

Pilate didn't know that standing right in front of him was the living, incarnate Truth. But being a relativist and acting on expedience, he had Jesus scourged, hoping this would satisfy the blood lust of those eager to see Him crucified. They robed Him in purple and put a reed in His hand and a crown of thorns on His brow. They brought Jesus out, and Pilate said, "Behold, the man," never knowing that He had answered his question, "What is truth?" Jesus said, "I am the way, the truth and the life. No one comes to the Father except through Me" (John 14:6)—and that is an absolute truth, my friends.

Look at Him. Behold Him. *Ecce homo.* Take a measure of the Man, Pilate says. We assess men today by their possessions, by their accomplishments. Jesus' friends and disciples had left Him. He had nothing that this world would count significant.

Pilate, at length, caved in and pusillanimously washed his hands before the multitudes, saying, "I am innocent of the blood of this just Person. You see to it" (Matthew 27:24b). So this judge of Rome turned over an innocent Man to be condemned while trying to absolve his own soul by the hypocritical act of washing his hands. So they mocked Jesus, they scourged Him, they put upon His shoulders that heavy Cross, and He started His final trek down the Via Dolorosa.

The women of Jerusalem came out to meet Jesus. Unlike that multitude of men who were filled with excitement and hateful glee as He started on His way to crucifixion, they did not mock Him or taunt Him, but rather they wept large tears of sadness and sorrow. Jesus stopped, turned, and said, "Daughters of Jerusalem, do not weep for Me" (Luke 23:28).

Jesus Christ never asked for anyone's pity. He never asked for anyone to weep for Him. He was not a victim. He was not a martyr. Jesus said in the Garden of Gethsemane, ". . . do you think that I cannot now pray to My Father, and He will provide Me with more than twelve legions of angels" (Matthew 26:53). (That translates to more than 72,000 angels.[13] That's amazing when you consider that *one* angel was able to slay 185,000 Assyrians in a single night.) Here was the great omnipotent God in human flesh. "[D]o not weep for Me."

Jesus never asked anyone to pray for Him. You ask, "What about there in the Garden of Gethsemane?" Jesus didn't ask them to pray for Him. He said, "Watch and pray, lest you enter into temptation" (v. 41). He said to the women of Jerusalem, ". . . weep for yourselves and for your children. . . . For if they do these things in the green wood, what will be done in the dry?" (Luke 23:28, 31). Indeed, that dry tree came for Jerusalem when the armies of Titus and Vespasian circled it and starvation came, so that women were eating their own children in Jerusalem. There was weeping and lamenting in those days.[14]

SIN BRINGS TEARS

"[W]eep for yourselves." One of the inevitable results of sin is tears. I assure you that for every sin you have ever committed, you shall weep. You will either weep tears of repentance and sorrow in this life, or you will weep tears forevermore in that place of darkness where there is weeping and wailing and gnashing of teeth forevermore. Sin brings tears, dear friend. Have you wept those tears of repentance as you have looked upon Christ?

When the soldiers had finished their ghastly work of affixing Jesus to the Cross like an owl skewered to a barn door, He hung there naked before the taunting, mocking multitudes, agonizing in pain. We read that they sat down and watched Him there. Can you imagine how hard the hearts of those soldiers, whose life occupation was crucifying men, must have become and what flint-like souls they had? It seems that humans can become hardened to anything, no matter how evil.

We have traveled down the Via Dolorosa, and we have begun to see some of the key personalities involved in the passion. As the curtain opens on Part III, we will take a closer look at these personalities—beginning with the traitor who helped initiate the passion.

PART III

PERSONALITIES IN THE PASSION

CHAPTER 6

JUDAS THE BETRAYER

Then Judas, who was betraying Him, answered and said,
"Rabbi, is it I?" He said to him, "You have said it."

MATTHEW 26:25

TRISKAIDEKAPHOBIA. DO YOU HAVE IT? It's very common—has been for 2,000 years. In case you don't recognize it, it comes from the Greek. *Tris* means "three"; *kai* means "and"; *deka* means "ten"; and *phobia* means "fear." So it is the fear of the three and ten, or the fear of thirteen.

It is a very common phobia. If you doubt it, just think about this. You just got your airline ticket, and you find that you are taking off from gate 13 and you are seated in row 13. Does that impact the way you feel? Actually, you might find that in many airports there is no gate 13, and in many airplanes there is no thirteenth row. We are really not superstitious are we?

How often we hear it said that back in the old days of the Bible times, people were superstitious, but not today. Why, we are enlightened, we are educated, we know better than that sort of thing. Just look at the Library of Congress. When you go there, you see the greatest, largest collection of human knowledge that does or has ever existed anywhere on this globe. About twenty-one or twenty-two million volumes was the count the last time I was there. Yet, nearby this vast array of human enlightenment, if you ask for a room in the hotel on the thirteenth floor, you will learn that they have no thirteenth floor. Similarly, many skyscrapers omit the thirteenth floor (at least in name). We may not be quite as enlightened as we thought.

But now NASA certainly feels that those there are enlightened. In fact, when it came to the shuttle flight, Flight 13, they decided they were going to call it 13. They weren't going to skip over to 14. Furthermore, they were going to launch on the thirteenth day of the month, and they were going to launch the shuttle at 1:13 in the afternoon. In military parlance that is 13:13. They are scientists, they said, not superstitious people. So, they began the countdown, and they got quite close to the launch. Suddenly there was a total power failure in the launch center, and the flight had to be scrapped. I'm not superstitious, I don't think, but I did find that interesting. I'm sure you do, too.

I think maybe the French are a little more superstitious than others. They have something called *quatorziemes*. A *quatorzieme* is a very accommodating kind of person. You see, if the seating list for a dinner should get stuck at thirteen, the *quatorzieme*, which means fourteen, are always ready to come in and break that deadlock and get rid of the thirteen. I guess that is one way to get a date—become a *quatorzieme*.

Where did this phobia of "13" come from? It came from the subject of this chapter, from Judas. He was, of course, the last disciple to be mentioned, always referred to as "Judas, who betrayed the Lord." So there at the Lord's Supper he was, as always, with the disciples and Christ, the thirteenth person. That has been considered a very ominous and unlucky thing ever since. To be one with this monster of iniquity was not something anyone wanted to do. Of course, Jesus was crucified on Friday. Combine the unlucky number of 13 with Friday and you have Friday the thirteenth.

Many names today are taken from the Bible. We have innumerable Pauls and Peters and Johns and Jameses and Davids, but I don't know anyone named Judas. There may be someone, but I don't think I have ever met anyone in my life named Judas. What mother would name her child Judas? None that I know; yet the name was a great name to begin with. It comes from Judah, which was the most prominent of the twelve tribes of Israel. The name means "praise." Ah, but the name has been dragged in the mud. It has gone down in history—a name in infamy—

as all such names do when they are connected with notorious individuals.

In 1939 there were 23 families listed in the New York phone directory named Hitler. In 1945 there were none. They either all changed names or they left town. I don't know which, and I don't know how leaving town would have helped their situation. Adolf was also a very common name in Europe in 1930, but it is not so anymore.

A GUIDED TOUR THROUGH HELL

How would you like to have a guided tour of Hell? If so, I would recommend that you read that great medieval classic Dante's *Inferno*, for that is precisely what he does. He takes you on a guided tour of Hell. It was a very influential book in the Middle Ages.

Today, most moderns feel that Hell has been evaporated. However, such is not the case. It matters not what we think or do not think about the subject; it stands ever the same.

As Dante takes us farther and farther into the depths of the pit, he shows different kinds of sinners—those who are guilty of the sins of lying or stealing or fornication or adultery or murder. Finally, he gets down to the very nethermost part of Hell. There, in the center, and all around him, are those who have betrayed their benefactors—who, as far as Dante is concerned—are the worst of sinners.

In the centermost place of that nether part of Hell is the gigantic fiend himself, Satan, who betrayed his great benefactor—God. This giant fiend has, within his great jaws, the figure of a man who Dante tells us, "kicks his leg on the fiery chin and has his head inside." Who is he? He is Judas Iscariot, the great betrayer of Jesus Christ—ever dying, ever living, ever suffering for ghastly sin.

That is how Judas was seen in the Middle Ages—in fact, all through history, up until recent times. Today, we have many who are engaged in the rehabilitation of bad reputations. Men who have stood for centuries in the pillory of history are now taken down, retried, burnished, dusted, and set upon a pedestal instead of a pillory for the admiration of all mankind. They say, "There really is no such thing as a bad boy, or a bad man. The problem is we just have misunderstood their motives. John Dillinger, you see, was just trying to provide for his aged mother, who wasn't well."

Of course, Judas has not been omitted. They would probably say, "There has been a terrible and gross mistake and misunderstanding— this dear man. . . ." One of the people who "understood" Judas was the man who wrote that ghastly, blasphemous film *The Last Temptation of Christ*. In that film, there is one hero, and that hero is not Jesus. It is Judas—portrayed as the only intelligent, respectable, sober-minded, down-to-earth individual in the midst of a bunch of extremist fanatics.

Judas is pictured as a superpatriot in this film and a man who came to see that Jesus had a problem—He was a dreamer; He was a vacillator. He had his opportunities to get rid of the Romans and stir up the people, and He failed them, one after another. What He really needed, you see, was a precipitator, and Judas was just the man to precipitate Him into action. So, Judas devised his whole plot with the single purpose of getting Jesus off dead center to exercise His amazing, miraculous power, overthrow the Romans, and set the nation free. You see, Judas was really very much like George Washington. He was a hero. We should put him on a pedestal and emulate him.

That is *not* the way it was. The Scriptures tell a very different story. The Bible says, very simply: Judas was a thief. He carried the bag, Christ's bag, that contained money collected for the food and the welfare of Christ and the Apostles and to meet the needs of other poor. He pilfered from that bag; he was a thief. He was no different than thousands of other thieves who have come and gone. In fact, what he did, because it was the bag of Christ, was such a sacrilege on top of a thievery that most thieves would recoil from such a ghastly deed.

JUDAS WAS WARNED

Jesus had warned Judas a number of times. A year before Christ's death, He said to His disciples: "Did I not choose you, the twelve, and one of you is a patriot." Did Jesus say that? No. He did not. Rather, he said, "Did I not choose you, the twelve, and one of you is a devil?" (John 6:70). Later, John says, "For He knew who would betray Him; therefore He said, 'You are not all clean'" (John 13:11).

Jesus warned Judas some months before when He said, "beware of covetousness" (Luke 12:15). Judas had to know that Jesus knew what was in his heart, yet he still plunged deeper into the depths of his depravity—even as we in our sin have known that God sees and knows what we are doing. For many that is not even a deterrent. When Judas went to the high priest, his motive was very clear. He said, "What are you willing to give me if I will deliver Him to you?" (Matthew 26:15).

Judas' problem was very simple; it was a matter of covetousness. His heart was held in the grip of gold. It is a terrible thing, not when a man has gold, but when gold has a man, and Judas was had by gold. He was a man who was consumed with avarice, and this was to lead to his utter destruction.

Avarice is a terrible sin and it has led to almost every other kind of sin imaginable. Were it not for avarice, most of the sins we see today would not occur:

- Prostitution is fed by avarice and the desire for gain.
- So is the great problem of drugs.
- So also is the problem of alcohol, which, like other drugs, has consumed the lives of countless millions.
- Gambling—the god of the covetous man—is there because people have this consuming avarice within them that causes them to even go to the extent of losing everything they have to get more gold.
- This is also true of pornography—whether we think of the pornography magazines in the stores or pornograpic movies on the screen, or soft-core pornography as seen on many of our television programs today that push the envelope. The produc-

ers that make it and the stations that show it are consumed with avarice; they are doing it for money.

There is hardly any sin at all that people will not do for money. Men sell their hearts and women sell their bodies for money. So Judas was thus consumed.

A MERE PAWN?

If Judas cannot be made into a patriot, there are others who would make him into nothing more than a pawn. "Oh, that poor guy. He didn't have a chance," said one coed. "It was predetermined that he was going to do what he did. In fact, the Bible prophesies that Judas was going to betray Christ, so what chance did he have? He was nothing but a pawn in a divine scheme." What shall we say to that? The Bible does prophesy that Judas was going to betray him. Right? Wrong. It never says that. It says in the Old Testament that Christ would be betrayed by a friend—

- by a friend who would lift his heel against Him,
- by a friend who would sell him for thirty pieces of silver,
- by a friend who would cast that money down, and the money would be used to buy a potter's field for graves for the poor,
- by a friend that would dip his hand in the dish with Him.

That person is never named, and when Jesus, at the Last Supper, says, "Assuredly, I say to you, one of you will betray Me" (Matthew 26:21), nobody knew who it was. They all, each one, said, "Lord, is it I?" No one suspected Judas. Judas was an impeccable hypocrite. He must have been highly regarded, because they chose him to be the treasurer. You don't just give your wallet or your purse to somebody willy-nilly. It has to be somebody you trust. I have no doubt that if Judas had applied for membership in one of our churches, he would have been received without any qualms. He probably could have gotten elected as an elder. Some churches might even make him the treasurer of the church. He was the treasurer for the twelve.

It is interesting, I think. We know that Matthew was a tax collector. We know that Peter and John were fishermen. But what did Judas do before he became an apostle? It doesn't say. Happily, it doesn't say, because if it did, it would put a stigma on that occupation forever. He was obviously a respected man because of what he was chosen to do, but he wore the mask. He was a hypocrite. That, of course, is a sin.

Today, for many of the moderns, it is the only sin that remains. It is no longer wrong or sinful to commit adultery or homosexuality or fornication or pornography or any of those things. There is nothing wrong with that. There is only one sin left and that is hypocrisy. How many times you have heard people say, "Oh, I'm not going to church. The church is filled with hypocrites." Well, you don't hear it said often that the bank is full of hypocrites, or the army is full of hypocrites, or the insurance company is full of hypocrites. It is always the church. In a certain way that is a backhanded compliment, because Christ has set such a high standard for us that it is much easier to fall short in the church. Someone said it is better to spend some time with hypocrites in the church than to spend eternity with them in Hell.

What is a hypocrite? It is a person that wears a mask. Remember the Greek dramas? They had masks on sticks. Acting hadn't been developed yet and so when they wanted to be sad, they had a mask with a mouth turned down, and when they were happy, they had one with the mouth turned up. Hypocrites do it without masks. Are we guilty of hypocrisy? Do we always do what we say? Do our teaching and our lifestyle match? I am afraid we are all guilty of some hypocrisy.

Of course, Judas's greatest sin was his betrayal of Christ. Here he joins Benedict Arnold, who was George Washington's dear friend. Washington brought him up through the ranks and made him a brigadier general, and yet he turned his back, betrayed him, and tried to turn West Point over to the British. His name has also gone down in the halls of infamy, as is true of Brutus. You don't hear of many people named Brutus anymore. It is a common name for a dog. "*Et tu, Brute?*" said Caesar when he saw his friend's dagger join all of the rest. At the sight of that, Caesar quit his struggle. "Thus falls Caesar," he said, as he collapsed and died. Brutus is close to that place in Dante's *Inferno* where Satan chomps on Judas.

But the greatest of the betrayers is that one who betrayed the Savior and Redeemer, Judas Iscariot. He walked with the King of Heaven and ended up in the pit of Hell. He had his chances. He came from a great tribe, Judah, the most eminent of the twelve. He had a great teacher in Jesus Christ—the greatest that ever lived. He had good acquaintances in the disciples. He had all of his needs met, and yet it was still because of covetousness that he was led, step-by-step, until finally he betrayed the Lord Himself—the greatest tragedy.

Could he have repented and trusted Christ and been forgiven? Yes, he could have. Remember, Peter denied Christ thrice, and yet he repented and turned to the Lord and was forgiven and went on to a glorious career. This could have happened to Judas, but he didn't believe, and he didn't really repent.

You say: Doesn't the Scripture say that Judas repented? It does. But there are two Greek words for repent. One is the true word for genuine repentance that leads to salvation, which is *metanoéo,* a change of the mind leading to a change of the heart and life. The other is the word that is used of Judas, which is simply *metaméllomai.* Judas was simply sorry.

There is no doubt that when he saw what they did to Christ, he was sorry for what he had done. He went into the temple and took the thirty pieces of silver, the price of a slave, and threw it down in the temple. How must the priests have laughed at him after he left, because he sold Christ for the price of a slave. They would have given almost anything he asked to get Him. I have often marveled at how little people are willing to sell their souls for. Remember, Judas didn't sell Jesus. What he sold was his own eternal soul for thirty pieces of silver—a week's wages.

When he saw Christ, he was indeed sorry. He said, "I have sinned by betraying innocent blood," and his newfound friends in the priesthood said, mockingly, "What is that to us? You see to it!" They laughed at him.

Then Judas went out. He could have gone "to the Cross," to this One that was hanging upon a tree suffering for our sins. However, (like so many today say, "Oh, God could never forgive me. You don't know how bad I've been"), he didn't really believe there was grace and forgiveness for him That is what Judas said, so he went out and hanged himself, probably on a tree that had a branch hanging out over the wall. After hanging himself, the rope broke and he fell a long distance to the rocks below and burst asunder.

Judas's final error was that he went to the wrong tree—the tree of death. He should have gone to the Tree of Life. Whoever you are, whatever you have done, however grievous or heinous your sins, there is mercy at the Cross. Remember, Jesus had just forgiven those who had nailed His hands and feet.

Someone once observed that suicide is the ultimate expression of despairing unbelief. Judas believed there was no hope. That is why the contrast between Judas and Peter, who returned to the Lord after he denied Him, is so instructive. There is pardon and mercy with the Lord for those who will confess, repent, and ask God to cleanse and renew them and make them whiter then snow.

When we observe the Lord's Supper, we take in our hands the tremendous symbols of that dying love—the broken body and shed blood of Christ—even as Jesus took the sop and dipped it into the dish and placed it into the mouth of Judas—an act of infinite love reserved for the special beloved guest. It was the last act of Judas before he went out to betray Christ. John said so much so succinctly, when he said, "And Judas went out and it was night." Ah, my friends, the betrayal of Christ leads to a lonely darkness—a darkness that will go on forever and forever in that outer darkness reserved for all of those who do not turn to Him.

The story of Judas cries out to us to be aware of the seductive power of sin. Through the power of His passion, Jesus has broken the power of sin, if we will but go to Him—before and after we fall.

CHAPTER 7

"I AM CAIAPHAS"

*And one of them, Caiaphas, being high priest that
year, said to them, "You know nothing at all, nor
do you consider that it is expedient for us that
one man should die for the people, and not
that the whole nation should perish."*

JOHN 11:49-50

I DON'T KNOW WHY I AM HERE TODAY. I did not want to come. I don't
know why I should be bothered with the likes of you. I'm not accus-
tomed to associating with the riffraff, but I was summoned; I had no
choice. I was supposed to tell you about those tumultuous days. Well,
I will at least take this opportunity to set the record straight, since you
have been misled by your vain superstitions. You will know the truth.
However, do not suppose that I have any illusions that what I say will
make much difference in your opinions, blinded as you are by your
prejudice and vain superstition, but I will at least state the facts as they
are, and as I understand them to be. Of course, as I understand them
to be is the only way they are, for these are the facts.

You should understand that I am the one. There was no other. You
prattle about this Judas, or this Pontius Pilate, but what are they? Mere
puppets . . . pawns. . . instruments in my hands. I conceived the whole
thing. I planned it, I executed it, and I carried it through. No one but
me. Yes, I was the mastermind behind the whole thing, and I carried it
off brilliantly. You see, I am a Sadducee, and we Sadducees are men of
the world—men of power. We don't argue. We act.

Do you know what it means to be the ruler of your people? Well, that is what I am. Do you understand what it means to be the high priest of Israel? I don't suppose you do. I don't know if it's worth the effort to try to enlighten you, but at least you will have the pleasure of knowing me better, and that, indeed, is a high privilege.

My name, of course, is Caiaphas—Joseph Caiaphas. Though you probably are not aware of it, Caiaphas is but another form of a name you are probably more familiar with—Cephas. One of your co-religionists (I believe his name was Simon) was surnamed Cephas as well. Cephas means "a stone," and that is exactly what I am. I am Caiaphas, the Stone of Israel.

My spies tell me that while I was condemning Him [Jesus] in the great hall of the Sanhedrin, that outside, your Cephas was denying that he ever even knew the man. Thus it was that Simon Cephas—Simon Peter, as you call him—the nether stone, and I, Joseph [Caiaphas] Cephas, the upper stone, ground your Jesus into dust. Between his denial and my condemnation, He was crushed.

I know some of you have said He was but the wheat that fell, and we but crushed Him into the flour that made the Bread of Life. Thus He came to Bethlehem, the House of Bread to be. Well, that is all poetry. I deal in facts in the real world, and He was crushed to death.

We leave it to the Pharisees, those quibblers, to talk about details of theology and the minutia of the law. We, the Sadducees, are the advanced thinkers. We, of course, take our name from the great Zadok, the high priest in David's day. We are what you would call the liberal-minded ones. We don't believe all of this nonsense, this superstition about angels and spirits and resurrections and Heaven and Hell.

Oh, we're still around. We are in your colleges and seminaries. We speak from your pulpits. You just don't know us by the name "Sadducee" any longer. However, we don't believe this foolishness. We are modern men, men of the age, men of enlightenment. There is no Heaven and no Hell. This is the Golden Age, and we have most of the gold. As far as Hell is concerned, we mete it out to those who oppose us. What need I, the high priest of Israel, with any Heaven, and what should I fear of any Hell? These are but the ignorant superstitions of a past age. As I said, we leave it to the Pharisees to quibble about theology.

I know some of you have said that I have the glittering eyes of a snake. Well, I care not what you think of me, but that might not be a bad picture for, you see, we watch things carefully. We do not act, we merely watch, and until this . . . this Nazarene became a threat, we did nothing at all. He did not disturb me in the least.

But the occasion for these tumultuous acts of which I speak happened just outside the gates of Jerusalem, but an arrow's flight away in Bethany. Some of the Pharisees came rushing into my apartment declaring that this Jesus had actually raised some man from the dead. Lazarus was his name.

Well, there is no resurrection. How do I know there is no resurrection? It's very simple. I do not believe there is a resurrection; therefore, there is no resurrection. I am the high priest of the Jews, and that settles it. Practical man that I am, though, I knew such superstitions could indeed cause trouble among the masses, and these foolish Pharisees were arguing among themselves. They were wringing their hands and saying, "What shall we do? For this Man works many signs. If we let Him alone like this, everyone will believe in Him, and the Romans will come and take away both our place and nation" (John 11:47-48).

At length they had said something of practical value, for you see, my place was quite exalted. As the high priest and leader of the people, it was also quite profitable. Annas, my father-in-law and a former high priest, had established the custom of requiring that only the temple shekel could be used for the purchase of the sacrifices, and therefore the people had to change their common coins into temple coins before they could buy their sacrificial animals. Of course, it is only natural to understand that there was a "slight" fee charged for this service, and that slight fee has made me one of the richest men in all of Israel, and no man, no one, no person is going to take my place from me.

EXPEDIENCY

So I said to these bumbling Pharisees, "You know nothing at all," which, of course, was mostly true. "Nor do you consider that it is expedient for us that one man should die for the people, and not that the whole nation should perish" (John 11:49b-50). That has a nice ring to it, don't you think? I have often been described as being quite eloquent. A turn of a phrase, not easily forgotten, caught their imaginations.

"Yes . . . Yes," they said. "Correct. Expedient that one man should die for the people and not that the whole nation should perish. A capital idea."

Fortunate are these ignorant people that they have me for their leader. What would they do without me? Giving more of my excellent advice, I said, "However, not on the feast day, lest a tumult should be made, for there are so many of these fanatical Galileans in Jerusalem at this time."

They said, "But what about Lazarus?"

"Kill him, too. What's another peasant or two to me, the high priest of the people?"

Therefore, we laid our plans and decided that on another occasion we would catch Him, trap Him, and we would kill Him. Sometimes, they say, Providence smiles on us. Of course, I do not say that because I do not believe in such foolishness as Providence. However, it seems to me there are times when circumstance smiles upon us and this was just such a time.

I was in my residence when an officer came and said, "Sir, the Pharisees have said there is a man who wants to speak to you. He wants to talk to you, a man from Kerioth—Judas Iscariot. He wants to see you about Jesus." I was about to dismiss him when that name "Jesus" caught my attention.

"Well," I said, "show him in, by all means." So, as high priest, I graciously granted him an audience. Judas came into my presence, and it was obvious to see that he was extremely nervous. He was wringing his hands and looking furtively from side to side. Then he said to me: "What are you willing to give me if I deliver Him [Jesus] to you?"

Ah, we have Him. He has fallen into our hands. I said to him, "This is of little concern to us, but I will give you thirty pieces of silver." Can you imagine? Thirty pieces of silver. I would have given him a hundred times that, but he took it, fool that he was.

We laid our plans. We knew right where He was. This audacious Jesus was just outside the gate in the Garden of Gethsemane. We sent not only the Roman guard, but the temple guard, as well, to make sure nothing went awry. They captured Him with no problem and bound His hands. Of course, I had given instruction that they send Him first of all to my father-in-law, his eminence, the former high priest Annas— a very expedient thing to do.

I know you have condemned me as a man who lived by expediency only—that I had no principles at all. Do I deny that? Of course not. I am no fool like you are, like those Pharisees are. Expediency is the only thing that works in the real world. Principles are for paupers and dreamers and idealists. I am the ruler of a state, and so it was, indeed, by expediency that I made all of my decisions.

Don't look at me like that. If your place, your job, your profession were endangered by living up to one of your so-called principles of this Jesus that you profess to follow, how many of you would immediately resort to expediency to save your own neck?

HYPOCRISY

So, they took Jesus to Annas, my dear father-in-law, who had made me wealthy by his provision for the money changing. Oh, please, not that . . . how many times have I heard that you have accused me of hypocrisy as well as expediency? You have said that I use religion for nothing but gain. I am so sick of that, and yet are there not some of you who have come to church for little other reason than that this would be a profitable place for you—professional man that you are, businessman that you are? How many deals have you worked out with contacts you have made right in church? Do not point the finger of hypocrisy at me.

Annas, of course, questioned Him well, as I knew he would. He asked Him first about His disciples, that others might be incriminated to cut this whole thing off, once and for all. However, Jesus would say nothing at all. Then he asked Him about His doctrine, that he might find something to accuse Him—not that Annas cared what His doctrine was any more than I do.

Jesus answered him: "I spoke openly to the world. I always taught in synagogues and in the temple, where the Jews always meet, and in secret I have said nothing. . . . Ask those who have heard Me what I said to them. Indeed they know what I said" (John 18:20-21).

One of the officers, infuriated and seeing the anger on the face of Annas, turned and struck Jesus in the face and said, "Do You answer the high priest like that?" (v. 22) This Jesus, I must give Him credit. He never was riled at all. Jesus answered him, "If I have spoken evil, bear witness of the evil; but if well, why do you strike Me?" (v. 23).

Annas could see that he would get nothing out of this prisoner, so he sent Him, bound, unto me. By this time, word had gone out all over the city, and we had gathered together the elders of the people, and the Sanhedrin was now meeting in the appointed hall.

At the appropriate moment, when all was prepared, Jesus was led in with his hands bound in front of Him. The bruise upon His cheek was still quite visible. He stood there looking first at one and then another of the counselors that sat in a great semi-circle in front of Him, while I sat in the center. He looked each one in the eyes. This was the first time I had ever personally seen the man. Again, I was struck with the serenity I had heard of before, but now witnessed for the first time.

He seemed not the least concerned. Did this fool not know His life was in jeopardy? I noticed, also, that as He looked into the eyes of the various counselors, immediately they averted His gaze and looked down to the ground. At length, He looked straight into my face with a look that seemed to send a shock through my body, right down to my soul. It was all I could do to keep from looking away, but leader that I was, I forced myself to continue looking at Him.

I said, "Bring in the witnesses." In they came, well prepared, we thought. But these bumbling dolts could not agree with themselves, and time after time, they contradicted one another, until it seemed like the entire trial would fall apart. Suddenly, a brilliant stratagem came to mind. Leader that I was, I suddenly saw my way through all of these difficulties. I stepped down from my throne chair and said to Him: "I put You under oath by the living God: Tell us if You are the Christ, the Son of God!" (Matthew 26:63).

Brilliant. I had placed Him under oath. An oath means nothing at all to me, but I knew that to this fool it meant everything, and He would be forced to tell the truth. If He denied He was Christ, the Son of God, that would be the end of His mission, and I would have won. If He affirmed it, that would be the end of His life, and I would have won. Brilliant strategy. I know that down through the years, some have said that this man never really claimed to be the Messiah. Well, I, as high priest placed Him under oath, and what did He say?

Very calmly He said, "I am." "It is as you said" (Mark 14:62, Matthew 26:64). Then He had the audacity to say, after that, "Nevertheless, I say to you, hereafter you will see the Son of Man sitting at the right hand of the Power, and coming on the clouds of heaven" (Matthew 26:64).

With that, I shouted "Blasphemy! He has spoken blasphemy! What further need do we have of witnesses?" (Matthew 26:65). Then, to add a dramatic touch, I ripped my robe before them and said to my counselors, "What do you think?"

They all cried out: "He is deserving of death," and they descended upon Him. They smote Him in the face, they spat upon Him, and they ripped handfuls of His beard from His face.

I knew that my strategy would not fail. There was but one more obstacle to be overcome before the plan could be consummated, and that was Pontius Pilate. I had said, "Leave Pilate to me," but it seemed like Pilate lacked the backbone for this task. He came out and said, "I find no fault in this man." We had stirred up the mob to cry for His blood, and they were shouting, "Crucify Him! Crucify Him!"

Pilate said, "Why, what evil has He done?" (Matthew 27:23).

I could see that again we were about to lose Him once more. Again, my prepared stratagem worked and worked magnificently. I knew Pilate had one weakness, one vulnerable spot. His position, his place, was due entirely to the will of Caesar, who had appointed him and who he considered his friend. Therefore, at the proper moment, I cried out from the back of the crowd, "If you let this Man go, you are not Caesar's friend" (John 19:12). I could see Pilate crumble—and he turned Jesus over to be crucified. Brilliant. Magnificent strategy.

We went back to my residence. I gathered some of my friends, and we had a delightful afternoon congratulating ourselves. Of course, I deferred to their congratulations saying, "Well, it was not I. We all acted together."

However, about three o'clock, suddenly it seemed there was a trembling of the ground, and that trembling grew until it was a roar. We rushed to the temple and into the Holy Place, and there we looked toward the Holy of Holies and saw that the great veil that separated the Holy of Holies from the Court of the Priests had been rent in twain. Someone came running into the temple and said this had taken place at the very moment the Galilean had died.

Nonsense. Just coincidence; nothing more. A mere coincidence. I did not believe in such miraculous interventions. Yes, I know you have said that even though I was the religious leader of the people, that I was an unbeliever. You have accused me of infidelity, as well as hypocrisy and expediency. Well, what is that to me? Those are super-stitions for the masses. I don't believe any of those things, and I will not stand to have some of you point your finger at me, either—some of you who do not believe in the basic tenets of your faith. Some of you profess, and yet, you do not really, in your hearts, believe many of these things to be true. How dare you point your finger at me.

The days went by peacefully until, on the third day there came a rumor. Then, after that, the guards rushed into the hall and said this Man had risen from the dead. After I was able to silence them and get some coherent story, they said that an angel had rolled back the giant stone from the tomb, and He had walked out alive. That was the most arrogant nonsense I have ever heard in my life. There are no angels and there is no resurrection. We Sadducees believe in no such nonsense as this.

However, if this story were to get out among the people, there could be no end of trouble. His dying would be more trouble than His living, so again I conceived of a brilliant plan. I asked for money to be brought in, and I gave a large sum to the soldiers. Their eyes got as big as saucers. I said to them, "Say no more of this to anyone, or else you will answer to me, but rather, say this: 'His disciples came at night and stole His body while we slept.' And if this comes to the governor's ear, we will appease him and make you secure" (Matthew 28:13-14). So, they went away, delighted to do just that—and I am happy to say that to this very day that story is still told and believed by many.

INFIDELITY

That was not the end of it. Reports kept coming. He had been seen here and there and another place. Finally, over five hundred people had seen Him in Galilee. Others had seen Him rise into the sky and disappear into the clouds. If that were not bad enough, a few days later He was supposed to have come in a new form of a Holy Spirit, and there were thousands converted right there, practically at my front door. Then, five thousand more, until the whole city was filled with the sound of their talking.

Even many of the priests were converted. There seemed to be nothing we could do about it. Then, I came across one that I felt would be at least the kind of man who could stand up to this. His name was Saul. Though he was a Pharisee (we'll forgive him for that), he had that intense zeal, that brilliance, so that he could understand what I understood. He hated these Christians as much as I did. He determined to go even to Damascus to bring them back bound in chains. I thought that would be an example to these here in Jerusalem. To my utter astonishment, he was hardly gone a few days when the report came back that he was there in Damascus preaching about this Jesus being the divine Son of God. Is there no one that can stand?

That teaching has now spread all over the world, even to ignorant peasants like you. I suppose little I have said will change your opinions of me. But that does not disturb me.

Yes . . . yes . . . I understand. I must go. I am being summoned again. Yes, that is wonderful. Yes, God. I am delighted. They have a place for me. That pagan procurator removed me from my place, and then the Romans came and destroyed our nation. All that I had tried to save, they destroyed. But now . . . now they have a place again for me. A place. That's what I need—a place. Judas, it is said, went to a place, and now there is a place for me.

Why are you binding my hands? my feet? Leave them alone. What are you going to do? Where . . . Where is my pl . . . No. That cannot be. There is no such place as Hell. It does not exist. Why are you lifting me? What have I done? You do not understand. I am Caiaphas! I am the high priest. I cannot be cast into Hellllllll . . . .

PETER: ROCK OR SAND?

*But Peter said, "Man, I do not know what you are
saying!" Immediately, while he was still speaking, the
rooster crowed. And the Lord turned and looked at
Peter. Then Peter remembered the word of the
Lord, how He had said to him, "Before the rooster crows,
you will deny Me three times." So Peter
went out and wept bitterly.*

"A ROCK? A ROCK, YOU SAY." The words seem to drip with scorn as they fall from the lips of that other Simon in the apostolic band: Simon Zelotes—Simon the Zealot, Simon the archpatriot. "Why," he continued, "to call Simon, the son of Jonas, a rock, is . . . is . . . is to insult rocks terribly."

Maybe it is that weakness in Simon Peter that causes all of us to like him so much, and perhaps all too often to emulate him—or at least, I do. It seems to me that Simon Peter sort of hops around through the New Testament on one foot, with his other foot tucked neatly in his mouth. He has this incredible knack of always saying the wrong thing at the right time.

Do you remember there on the Mount of Transfiguration, when Christ appeared with His glory, glistening in His clothes, as His being shone through His garments, and the apostles who were with Him saw something of His divinity? Well, Peter just had to make a speech. Peter's name, Simon, (Simeon, in Hebrew), meant "one who hears; to listen; to understand." He was wrongly named by his parents; "Peter, the Mouth" would have been a better name. "Then Peter answered and said to Jesus, 'Rabbi, it is good for us to be here; and let us make three tabernacles: one for You, one for Moses, and one for Elijah'" (Mark 9:5). "[A]nd a voice came out of the cloud, saying, 'This is My beloved Son. Hear Him!'" (v. 9:7b)—which is heavenly politeness for, "Shut up, Peter, and listen."

BOAST NOT

Or do you remember that time in the Upper Room, when Jesus took off His garment, clothed Himself with a cloth, and began to wash the feet of the disciples? When He came to Peter, "Peter said to Him, 'You shall never wash my feet!' Jesus answered him, 'If I do not wash you, you have no part with Me.' Simon Peter said to Him, 'Lord, not my feet only, but also my hands and my head!'" (John 13:8-9).

"The feet will be sufficient, Peter."

Peter was always saying the wrong thing at the right time. Peter is, in many ways, a negative example. He provides a very powerful example of what not to do, as he moves toward the precipice of his great apostasy.

Near Atlanta, Georgia, there is a tourist attraction known as Stone Mountain. It is a huge stone that looks like it fell right out of Heaven. It has a gradual incline on one side that goes up several hundred feet and levels off at the top. From there, it begins on the other side a gradual declension for a hundred feet or so, and then drops suddenly, precipitously, hundreds of feet to the rocks below.

A number of people over the years, wanting to get close to the edge to get a better view, have suddenly found their feet slipping out from under them and they fall on their backs. They begin to slide, grabbing for weeds or crevices of some sort. Unable to stop themselves, they gather speed, until with a great scream, they plunge into the air and down to their deaths. The Park Services has built a barrier up at the top to keep people from even starting down that dangerous declension.

I think we ought to notice the dangerous decline down which Peter began—a slippery slope that led to his apostasy. There are some great lessons to be learned from reading the life of Peter, some of which we should *not* emulate.

Peter's problems all began with a boast: "Even if all are made to stumble because of You, I will never be made to stumble" (Matthew 26:33). "Even if I have to die with You, I will not deny You!" (v. 35). He lifted himself up just a little bit higher than the rest of the rabble.

The Bible tells us that pride goes before destruction and a boast before a fall. I have discovered over the years that that is incredibly true. It seems to be infallibly true in my life. Not only does it seem to me that every time I boast of anything, I shortly thereafter fall flat on my face, but all I have to do is even think it and it happens.

One example of that stands out clearly in my mind. Many years ago, I was invited to speak at the Pensacola Theological Institute. During some free time, I was invited to go out to one of their beaches. On this particular day, tremendous waves were thundering and crashing upon the shore. Someone exclaimed, "Oh, I'm not going to go out in the water with waves like that."

I didn't say a word, but I thought to myself, "Hah, I've never seen a wave yet that is going to keep me out of the water. Didn't I grow up fifty yards from Lake Michigan? Wasn't I a lifeguard in camp? Didn't I spend eight years scuba diving in the ocean? Why, there hasn't been a wave born that's going to keep me on dry land."

So I put on my fins, my mask and snorkel, and I started out into the water, diving through one wave after another, going out farther and farther, until I was at the place where I could take on one of these waves and ride it magnificently to the shore.

Finally, there came a huge wave. It must have been about ten feet high. What I didn't know was that there was also a tremendous riptide going out on the surface of the water. That is why, when the wave picked me up and dropped me down, the riptide pulled me back out, turning me upside down. This huge wave slam-dunked me on the sand below. Then it dribbled me into the shore. I was head over heels, side over side, upside down. I had absolutely no control whatsoever.

Finally, it spat me out and I exploded to the surface to get some air, and then rushed out of the water, lest another one of those monsters got a hold of me. I found that my snorkel was gone altogether; my mask was backward around my neck; one fin was up around my knee, and the other one was gone completely. The first thought that came to my mind, was, "Hah, there hasn't been a wave born yet that's going to keep me out of the water."

Boasting goes before a fall. Peter was also going to learn that lesson the hard way.

SPIRITUAL NEGLECT

The second step Peter took down that slippery slope toward apostasy was neglect—spiritual neglect. Do you remember what Jesus said that night in the Garden of Gethsemane? He said, "Watch and pray, lest you enter into temptation" (Mark 14:38a).

Peter couldn't watch and he couldn't pray . . . but he *could* sleep. When Jesus came back from praying, He said, "What! Could you not watch with Me one hour?" (v. 40). Another hour passed with the same result; and the third hour—again the same result.

Peter neglected the means of grace and became spiritually weaker and weaker and weaker. Like Peter, when we neglect the means of grace—e.g., prayer, Bible study, and Christian fellowship—we lose our immunity to resist sin. When confronted by some great temptation, we will find that our strength has fled from us and we will be overwhelmed and brought into more trouble than we ever thought possible, because we have neglected the means of grace.

IMPETUOSITY

The third footstep Peter etched in that slippery slope was the step of impetuosity. Waking from his sleep, he found Christ surrounded by armed men. He leaped to his feet, great hulk of a man that he was, drew his sword to cleave one of the soldiers in half, but with sleep in his eyes, perhaps, he missed him and took but his ear off with a mighty blow.

Jesus told him to put away his sword, and then He restored the man's ear—even though this man was sent there as part of a group to arrest Him. In the movie, *The Passion of The Christ*, it powerfully shows how Christ's healing act must have had a powerful impact on that man.

Back to Peter and his impetuosity. How many times we try to serve the Lord without having prepared that service with prayer. We try to witness for Christ without praying, without preparing our hearts, without cleansing ourselves to handle holy things. How totally fruitless will be that type of ministry.

The great preacher, E. M. Bounds, said that unless a sermon has been properly bathed in prayer, however beautiful, however articulate, it is like taking a handful of pearls and throwing them out onto black soil, expecting that they are going to take root and bear fruit. They just lie there and glitter, dead and useless, and so was Peter's service.

PETER PANICKED

A fourth step Peter took down that slippery slope was that he panicked. He panicked and was filled with fear because he was not trusting in Christ. When we trust in our own selves and the power of our own arm or our own abilities or our own speaking to serve the Lord, we will find that to be utterly useless. Though self-confidence is heralded today as a great virtue, it is, indeed, a vice and sin; it is trusting and having faith in self.

We are to have faith in Christ. When we don't trust in Christ, but rather, trust in ourselves, we will attempt to do things in our own strength. We will discover there are some things bigger than we are that we can't do, and then we will turn to fear and despair and be overwhelmed. Self-confidence leads to pride on the one hand, when we succeed, and despair on the other hand, when we fail. So it was with Peter.

PETER FOLLOWED AFAR

The next step down that slippery slope for Peter was that he followed afar off. First, having panicked, he fled into the trees in the darkness. Finally, grabbing hold of the trunk of a tree, he whirled around to look back to see what was happening. No one was following him, but he could see in the glow of the torches that Christ was being led back to Jerusalem with His hands bound. Peter, perhaps out of guilt, perhaps out of curiosity, decided to follow . . . but not too closely.

How many reading this book do the same? You have religion, but you don't want to get too much. You don't want to get too close. You don't want to wear it on your sleeve. You don't want to be fanatical in your religion. You certainly don't want to talk about it in public, so you just follow afar off.

My friends, that is a very dangerous place. Not only is it dangerous, but also, it is deadly and dull. The Scripture says that "at thy right hand there are pleasures forevermore" (Psalm 16:11 KJV). However, when we follow afar off, we have just enough religion to make us miserable, but not enough to do us any good.

BECOMING "ONE OF THE BOYS"

So Peter, with the help of John, entered into the courtyard of the high priest, where they waited while Christ was taken inside to be tried. Peter made his last mistake before he was to plunge over the precipice of denial: he mixed himself in with the unbelievers. He sat among them around the fire, trying to look just like one of them—to be "one of the boys"—to enter in with the things of the world. "If you would just forget about all of those scruples, ole' friend, and do the things we do, then we'll not pay too much attention to your religion, because, by then, you will have convinced us that you are nothing but a hypocrite, like all of the rest. So we can accept you and we'll have a good time with you."

How many people seem to find their fellowship and their friendship with unbelievers. You say, "Wait a minute. Didn't Jesus go among unbelievers?" Yes, He did, but He went among them to minister to them and to give to them. There are too many in the Church who go among unbelievers constantly. They go out in the evening for a time of enjoyment with unbelievers, and they give them nothing at all—never a word of witness. They go to get, not to give. That's a very dangerous place.

The Bible says, "Come out from among them, And be separate" (2 Corinthians 6:17).

Yet those who find their joy and their friendship and their fellowship—their enjoyment with unbelievers—should remember that "birds of a feather flock together" in the spiritual world as well. You may ask yourself: Am I really any different from them at all?

PETER'S DENIAL

By now, Peter, having made his way down that slippery slope, is at the very edge of the precipice. He is to be confronted with that great temptation for which he is totally unprepared. The portress of the high priest, who watched him when he came in with John, noticed that he looked somewhat familiar. She walked over and looked at his face as the fire reflected off of his countenance. Finally she said, "This man was also with Him" (Luke 22:56b). "You are not also one of this Man's disciples, are you?" (John 18:17).

Peter, this is your great opportunity. "Though all men deny Him, yet will I never deny Him," you had said. Now is your opportunity. Now is your chance to confess Him. Remember what you said when Jesus asked the disciples who He was? You said, "You are the Christ, the Son of the living God" (Matthew 16:16).

Now, Peter, now . . . here is your chance to make the same confession—not in the midst of disciples, but in the midst of the unbelievers.

Peter, stand up and say, "Yes, yes, I was with Him. Yes, this is the Christ, the Son of the Living God."

That same question was being asked at the same time to Christ in the hall above. "Are You the Christ, the Son of the Living God?" asked the high priest, putting Jesus under an oath.

Jesus said, "It is as you said" (Matthew 26:64a).

Now, Peter, echo that confession. Be a man. Stand up. But Peter replies, "I do not know the Man!" (Matthew 26:72b).

"Peter, do you not know Me? Do you not remember, Peter, the first time we met and I said to you, 'You are Simon the son of Jonah. You shall be called Cephas (which is translated, A Stone)' (John 1:42). Have you forgotten that, Peter? Do you not remember at all? How can it be, Peter, that you say you never knew me?"

A short time later, someone else says, "This fellow also was with Jesus of Nazareth" (Matthew 26:71). His denial has now become easier. Sin always becomes easier as we move down that slippery slope toward disaster. Peter says rather facilely now, "Man, I don't know what you're talking about. I know not the Man."

"You don't know Me, Peter? Have you forgotten that time when the storm was so boisterous and you were in the ship with the disciples and I came walking to you on the sea? You said, 'Lord, if it is You, command me to come to You on the water,' and I said to you, 'Come,' and you stepped out of the ship. The liquid sea became solid under your feet and you walked toward me. Peter, have you forgotten that? (Matthew 14:26-31). Do you not know me, Peter?"

After an interval of about an hour, Peter—having walked out into the darkness where he could not be seen so clearly—has come back again, and once more is mingling with the unbelievers. Again, another man observes him very carefully, and then very earnestly declares, "Surely, you are one of them; for you are a Galilean, and your speech shows it" (Mark 14:70).

Peter leaps to his feet and says, "I do not know this Man of whom you speak! Do you think my speech betrays me as being one of them?

I'll show you speech which will convince you for certain that I'm not one of them." Peter begins to curse and to swear with all manner of foul fisherman's language that he thought he had put away. It comes flowing out again like an open sewer. He imprecates and vilely swears and uses all sorts of terrible words, and ends up by saying, "I KNOW NOT THE MAN!!"

CONVICTED BY A LOOK

Suddenly, from over the wall there comes an unmistakable sound. It is the sound of a cock crowing. Peter is stunned into silence. He looks up to the second floor, and there, with hands bound, Jesus is being led from one hall to the next, his face dripping with spittle. Jesus stops, turns, and looks at Peter—at least that is what the English text says. The Greek text says that He looked *into* Peter. Peter says to himself, "He heard what I said. He heard all of those foul words; He heard the blasphemy, He heard the cursing, He heard me say that I never knew Him at all."

"Peter, Peter. Could you not believe that I could hold you up in this hour of your trial? Do you not remember, Peter, when you saw me there upon the mountain in all of my glory, when my Deity shown through with such a brightness that you could hardly look upon it? Did you think I was so weak that I could not help you, Peter? Ah, Peter, are you a common stone upon which I must break my heart? Be not afraid; fear not, Peter, for in your final, your dreariest hour, you shall not be denied, as I am here. My voice shall be heard clearly, 'Let this man go, because I know him. Let him be cleared.'"

Peter suddenly turns, overwhelmed with emotion, and pushes through the crowd, out the door, and into the darkness, sobbing as if his heart would break and weeping with hot scalding tears running down his cheek. He goes out weeping bitterly. Peter has come to discover the meaning of repentance.

PETER REPENTS

Is it not sad that too many of us follow Peter in his declension, but we do not follow him in his repentance? Peter repented immediately. He didn't wait for hours or days or months or years. He repented bitterly with tears. Some people say they are afraid to speak because they are afraid they will weep. Ah, dear friend, be not afraid of that. Thank God if your heart has been softened to the place that you can weep.

One thing is absolutely certain: God in Heaven never weeps. The angels never weep. Animals never weep. It is left for fallen man alone to weep. Jesus, when in the flesh, wept over Lazarus, and He wept over Jerusalem. But it is only as man that anyone can weep.

There is one thing absolutely certain about sin—something that is absolutely inevitable: it will dissolve one day into tears—either into tears of repentance here, or tears of agony in that place where there is weeping and wailing and gnashing of teeth, where unbelievers shall weep unendingly through all the ages of eternity.

Have *you* wept for your sins? My dear friend, let me assure you of one thing: You most certainly will, either here or there, but you will weep for your sins. "Weep for yourselves," said Jesus.

Indelibly carved in the walls of my memory is that night when the Gospel of Christ became clear to me for the first time. I looked up at Calvary's hill, I saw that One hanging upon the Cross, and I knew that it was for my sins that He was agonizing and dying. I slipped off my easy chair onto my knees. With my head upon the carpet, I began to weep, to sob, to say, "Oh God, I'm sorry. I'm sorry. I didn't know." I began to weep for my sins. I began to weep like I had never done in my life before.

Have you wept for your sins? May it be here on earth so that you may enter into the tearless Heaven, where God shall wipe away every tear from our eyes. May we avoid the negative lessons of Peter's life and learn the positive one—that Peter came to repentance. Jesus met him later on the shore of the Sea of Galilee and said to him, "Simon, son of Jonah, do you love Me more than these?"

"Yes, Lord; you know that I love You."

"Simon, son of Jonah, do you love Me?"

"Yes, Lord; You know that I love You."

And a third time, "Simon, son of Jonah, do you love Me?" (John 21 16-17).

Simon was grieved that He had asked him three times, not realizing that Christ was giving him an opportunity to demonstrate the reality of his repentance, as three times he had denied Him, and now three times he affirmed his love. "Yes, Lord; You know that I love You."

QUO VADIS

For the rest of his life, Peter abundantly proved the sincerity of his repentance. He served the Lord in gladness, bringing His Word first to the Jews and then the Gentiles. The first several chapters of Acts chronicles what Peter did for Christ. He was certainly the first chief Christian witness until Paul came on the scene. Peter focused mainly on leading Jewish people to the Lord, while Paul focused on the Gentiles.

Rome, the city that opposed the Gospel at first, is today known as the city of Peter and Paul. The humble fisherman from Galilee, along with the former Pharisee and tentmaker, managed to turn that city upside down. The world has never been the same since.

Peter's repentance was seen even in his death. Speaking of Nero's persecution, *Foxe's Book of Martyrs* states:

> In this persecution, among many other saints, the blessed apostle Peter was condemned to death. He was crucified, as some write, in Rome. (However, others are not quite sure about that.) Hegesippus says that Nero sought Peter to put him to death. When the people learned of this, they begged Peter to flee the city. They were so insistent that he was finally persuaded. He started to leave, but coming to the gate, he had a vision of Jesus coming to meet him. He worshiped Him and said, "Lord, whither dost Thou go?" To which the Lord answered, "I am come again to be crucified." By this, Peter understood that he was supposed to suffer, so he returned back into the city. Jerome said that he was crucified upside down on his own insis-

tence because he was not worthy to be crucified in the same form and manner as the Lord was.[15]

Though Peter certainly had his moments where he became as shifting and as unreliable as sand, by the mercy of Christ he was able to live up to the meaning of his given name: Peter, which means "rock."

CHAPTER 9

"I AM PONTIUS PILATE"

*Then Jesus came out, wearing the crown of
thorns and the purple robe. And Pilate said to them,
"Behold the Man!"*

JOHN 19:5

YOU HYPOCRITES. YOU SUPERCILIOUS HYPOCRITES. I know what you've been saying about me—"coward," "compromiser." How empty those words sound coming from your mouths. You, who have done the very same thing over and over again that I did only once. Yes, I know about your kind. I have had the opportunity to meet many of them where I have been and from whence I come to speak to you today. I have come to talk to you today from Hell. I have come for several purposes. One of them is to set the record straight.

What do you know? What do you really know about it? You, who have passed your facile judgments on me and bandied my name about. Oh yes, they have brought me all of your reports. I know them well. But you weren't there. You don't know what it was like. Let me tell you a few things. I am a Roman of equestrian rank, of noble birth. Do you know what it was like to rule over those fatuous Jews—those recalcitrant rebels, ever stirring, never willing to submit themselves to the proper government of Rome? I was their supreme commander: Procurator of Judea, appointed by Tiberius himself. I was not an ordinary procurator: *I was Procurator Cuim Postatae,* not just in charge of finances, but also in charge of the military. I was the soldier in charge of the jurisprudence. I held within my hands the power of life and death. Do you know what that responsibility means?

From the very first moment I arrived, there was trouble stirring in that province which I had been honored to rule because of my diplomatic skills and firmness. When Tiberius was in Rome, I was in Judea—the representative of the emperor of the empire that ruled the world. Rome. Mighty, undefeatable Rome.

I had no sooner arrived in Jerusalem, but that city became filled with stories about one John, who was creating a stir out in the wilderness and causing whispers to fly throughout the city. The year was 26 A.D. as you now count time. I sent my spies; don't suppose that I didn't know. I had my finger on everything that took place in Jerusalem and in Judea. They reported everything he said, but this was not sedition.

Then, just a few months later, I heard other reports of one who was supposed to be the Messiah of Israel, the King of the Jews. Again, I had my intelligence—my spies were there on the Mount, by the river, and everywhere. This was not sedition. No, mighty Tiberius had nothing to fear from this itinerant preacher from Nazareth.

From the very beginning, my career in Judea was tied up with the tumultuous Jews who would not be ruled. All I did was simply command that the Legion enter into Jerusalem and, of course, they brought with them their ensigns, bearing the Roman eagle and the name Caesar. Why this was nothing at all. They had been in a thousand cities ten times over and no one had said anything—they had bowed to the imperial might of Rome. But not these Jews. No way. Why, the first thing I knew there were thousands of Jews in front of the palace protesting and demanding that the ensigns be removed from the Holy City. They said it was idolatry to have these eagles in Jerusalem.

I went out, spoke to them, and told them to disband. They would not. I waited patiently. For days they continued protesting, night and day. Finally, I fixed on my plan and sent hundreds of my soldiers out to mingle among them. Then I, myself, appeared and gave this order: "Either disperse immediately or you will be killed on the spot." With that signal, my soldiers drew their swords. What a stroke of genius. With that these pusillanimous Jews would flee to their homes, and they would now know something of the might of Rome.

Did they flee? Not them. They fell on their knees and exposed their necks and said, "Here, here, strike us here. We would rather die than allow this idolatry to continue." I was dumbstruck. I did not know what to do. I could not kill them all, so I called off my soldiers, retreated, and removed the ensigns from Jerusalem. Still not being satisfied, they sent an envoy to Rome and complained to Tiberius, himself. In due time, I received a rebuke from the emperor.

Not long afterward, I was planning to honor Tiberius, my benefactor, and ordered some beautifully made shields of gold hung in the palace of Herod. There were no eagles attached—nothing but the name of the donor and the name of Tiberius, in whose honor they were hung. Again, these same rebellious Jews came and protested that this, too, was blasphemy and idolatry. Another word was sent to Rome. The reply came back. I was certain that Tiberius would be proud of me, since I had desired to honor his name; but no, that was not the reply. It was: "Remove the shields to Caesarea, and don't let this happen again." You see, you knew nothing about this. No, you ignorant moderns pass your judgment so quickly. You do not know what it was like to rule a province such as that in the name of Rome. I knew clearly that one more complaint to Rome and I would be through.

It was against this backdrop that that Friday which you call "Good" held in it nothing good for me. Indeed, it approached me that morning with the most dreadful insignia of death and hopelessness. I was asleep, as any decent Roman would be. The sun had not even come up, and the captain of the guard awakened me to inform me that the Sanhedrin was outside demanding my presence.

I do not know which of the two I hate the more—to be awakened before sunrise, or to meet with the Sanhedrin. I cannot possibly think of a combination of events more absolutely obnoxious to my tastes. Yet, that is the way that day began. Further, I was told they would not even come into my palace, because they might be defiled in the presence of us heathens. Imagine. I, a noble, born a Roman equestrian—a heathen in their ill-bred half-barbarian eyes. Noble Roman that I was, I did go out to meet them and to do my duty as the representative of Caesar. There they were, not only the Sanhedrin, but also a motley mob of people swaying and surging behind them, with others joining them.

There, in front of them, stood the prisoner. He didn't look very dangerous to me. He looked more like one of their itinerant prophets, standing there with his hands bound in front of him and spittle dripping from his beard. Not a very impressive figure—hardly one that should demand my attention, especially before daylight. With great exasperation, which I tried my best to conceal, I said to them, "What accusation bring you against this man?"

Would you believe what their response was? I could not believe my ears. They said, "If he were not an evildoer, we would not have delivered Him up to you" (John 18:30b). As if they expected that I, Pontius Pilate, Procurator of Judea in the name of Tiberius Caesar, was in some way going to rubberstamp their judgment upon this man, without even hearing the facts of the case.

Well, they did not know me very well. Nor did they know anything about Roman law, which was to defend the weak and crush the proud. Returning their words in kind, I said to them, "You take Him and judge Him according to your law" (John 18:31).

Their response was instantaneous. "It is not lawful for us to put anyone to death" (v. 31). Those words did my soul good that early morning and brought a sense of warmth that took away something of the night chill. Yes, yes, you stiff-necked Sadducees. You have no right to put anyone to death because you are the conquered subjects of Rome, and we have kept in our hands the right of capital punishment.

If this were a capital crime, I would have to hear it. "What is the accusation?" They began to cry out, first one and then another, "We found this fellow perverting the nation, and forbidding to pay taxes to Caesar, saying that He Himself is Christ, a King" (Luke 23:2).

These were serious matters. At that time, I did not know what I have since learned in that place to which I soon went, that they had already tried Him for altogether other crimes than sedition. They had tried and convicted Him of blasphemy, because He claimed to be the Son of God. They well knew that Roman law contained no ordinance against blasphemy, much less as a capital offense. We, in Rome, who are broadminded and tolerant of all of the many gods, were about as likely to put someone to death for blasphemy as a modern American court would be to put someone to death for flying a kite.

On the spur of the moment, casting all judicial candor to the wind, they changed their accusation and accused him of that crime, which they knew would have the greatest weight in my eyes: the crime of sedition. Therefore, naturally, I had to examine the case. I returned to the palace and called the prisoner before me. He stood silently in my presence. For the first time in my life, I looked into those eyes. I tried to look away and found that I was transfixed by a gaze that seemed to penetrate deep into my soul. To ease the sense of uneasiness that came over me, I said to Him, "Are You the King of the Jews?" (Luke 23:3).

Would you believe that this man, bound and standing before me said: "Are you speaking for yourself about this, or did others tell you this concerning Me?" (John 18:34). As if I, the Roman ruler of Judea, should in some way be interested in some Jewish claimant to the throne of Israel. Why, if he were a king, he would simply be another one to crush under the heel of Rome.

I responded with a growing sense of exasperation: "Am I a Jew? Your own nation and the chief priests have delivered You to me. What have You done?" (v. 35).

Silence. Again, that look that seemed to reverse our positions. For a while, it felt as if I were standing before Him, as the prisoner of His law. Finally, He answered: "You say rightly that I am a King. For this cause I was born, and for this cause I have come into the world, that I should bear witness to the truth" (v. 37).

Ah, one of those. One of those fanatical preachers who builds kingdoms upon the clouds. This man is no traitor to Rome. This man is no threat to the throne of Tiberius. I responded: "What is truth?" You fool; do you not know that it is expediency that turns the world? Do you not know that might is right and truth? I left him and went back out to the praetorian and took my place upon the *bema* and said to the waiting multitude: "I find no fault in Him at all" (v. 38).

To my astonishment, rather than being satisfied with my judicial verdict, there was a great clamor and uproar. The Jews began to shout, "He stirs up the people, teaching throughout all Judea, beginning from Galilee to this place" (Luke 23:5). Did I hear correctly? Did you say *Galilee*? Is this man from Galilee? Ah, one as wise in the ways of the world as I would not pass up an opportunity such as that to dismiss the problem from my hands that early morning. This was not even within my jurisdiction. It was Herod's problem and Herod Antipas happened to be in Jerusalem that very hour for the Passover.

I thought to myself: Here is an opportunity to mend some broken fences and to heal some old wounds, because Herod had often complained that I usurped his authority. I sent the prisoner to Herod and that, thought I, was that.

I returned to my chamber and to my bed, although I must confess that for a while I had some difficulty getting to sleep. That gaze kept returning to my sight and troubled my thoughts. Finally, as I was about to drift off to sleep, *again*, incredibly, I was aroused by the guard and told they were back. The Sanhedrin was back. The prisoner was back. Like a bad penny, they had bounced back. What did Herod do? He sent a note expressing his pleasure that I had thought enough of him to send the prisoner for his inspection.

Well, at least one good thing happened. From that day on, Herod and I were friends. I know what some of you have said about that. I know how you have said that Herod and I could only get together in one thing: the rejection of the Son of God. How dare you. How dare you Americans say that about me? You, who have rejected Him from your schools. You have tried to reject Him from your government. You, who even tried to reject Him from the space and the moon that He created. You dare accuse me of rejecting Him. Hypocrites!

Let's get the record straight, shall we? I did not get to be procurator without having something of a fertile mind. It came to me at that moment that to curry the favor of these Jews and make them somewhat easier to rule, it had been my custom on the Passover to grant them the pardon of any prisoner they chose, so, I called for the most abominable character we had in our prisons who was awaiting execution. They brought him up. His name was Barabbas. He was a murderer, a traitor, an insurrectionist—all the things of which they accused Jesus. In fact, his first name was even Jesus.

I stood both of them before the people. There was Barabbas—filthy, vile, tough, mean. Next to him stood the serene, majestic Jesus of Nazareth. Obviously, the choice was clear, but I asked them, "Which of the two do you want me to release to you?" (Matthew 27:21).

To my utter amazement, with one voice the people cried out, "Barabbas!" I said to them, "What then shall I do with Jesus who is called Christ?" (v. 22).

They responded in the voice of a serpent: "Crucify Him!"

I asked: "Why, what evil has He done?" (v. 23). At that moment, a servant came and delivered a note to me from my wife which read: "Have nothing to do with that just Man, for I have suffered many things today in a dream because of Him" (v. 19).

I must confess to the feeling of awe that passed over me. I determined that, if at all possible, I would release this man; yet, these Jews were clamoring for his blood. Finally, I hit on one last expedient. I said to them, ". . . having examined Him in your presence, I have found no fault in this Man concerning those things of which you accuse Him; no, neither did Herod, for I sent you back to him . . . I will therefore chastise Him and release Him" (Luke 23:14-16).

I thought that was a brilliant compromise. Oh, indeed, it might not be thought worthy of an administrator and a judge to scourge one whom I had just declared innocent, but perhaps it would assuage the blood lust of these who were crying for His death.

I delivered Him to the lectors, who took Him and bound Him. They scourged Him with that Roman whip, bearing in its leather thongs the sharpened pieces of bone or metal. My soldiers, catching the spirit of the morning, found an old purple robe and threw it around His blood-soaked body. They put a broken reed into His hand, made a crown of thorns, and placed it upon His brow. They pushed Him, stumbling, back upon the Praetorium.

There He was—you could see the blood dripping from His hands and running down His ankles, and from His brow into His eyes. Certainly a sight to touch the hardest of hearts. I thought this would surely satisfy them and told the crowd, "Behold the Man!" (John 19:5).

Instead of being satisfied, they cried even louder, "Away with Him, away with Him! Crucify Him!" (v. 15).

I asked, "Shall I crucify your King?" In their final apostasy, they said, "We have no king but Caesar" (v. 15). I couldn't believe those words.

Just as I was determining in my mind that this is as far as I would go and was going to say to them, "I have tried Him, I have scourged Him and now I will set Him free"—I call upon whatever gods there may be that I was going to let him go—but then they said those fatal words: "If you let this Man go, you are not Caesar's friend. Whoever makes himself a king speaks against Caesar" (v. 12).

Ah, the *amicus Caesar,* "the friend of Caesar," was that relationship above all others upon this earth which I desired and which I prized. Surely another envoy would be off to Rome bearing the tale that I had set someone free who claimed to be a king and claimed to compete with Caesar. It would be my head.

Oh, but all of you have judged me. My job was at stake. How many of you have taken jobs where you have compromised what you claim to believe? I was no Christian. I didn't have your professed views, and yet you have jobs that call you to do things that you know are wrong; yet you stifle your conscience and go ahead. You have jobs that require you to work on your Sabbath, yet you stifle your conscience and go ahead. Don't you dare point your finger at me, you hypocrites. I had to contend with the Caesar of Rome. Who is your boss compared to him? Yes, I caved in. Just exactly like you would have done.

I had determined that I would not pass the sentence, and with a brilliant stroke of genius, I called for my servants to bring me a basin of water. I set the basin before them and said, "I am innocent of the blood of this just Person. You see to it" (Matthew 27:24). I would have nothing to do with it.

I call all of you to realize that I would not condemn Him myself. I told them that if they were so thirsty for His blood that they would have to do it. Yes, you, you bloodthirsty Pharisees, Sadducees, High Priests—nothing would suffice. Look at the man. Why will you not let Him go? No, you must have His blood—crucify Him yourself. I will have nothing to do with it. I am innocent, I tell you. I am innocent. I didn't do it. I am innocent. Do you not see? I am innocent. I am innocent of His blood. I am innocent, I tell you. You did it! You did it! You crucified Him. Not I. *You* did it!

I have come to warn you. I have come from far because some of you are doing exactly what I did. You see, I tried not to condemn Him, but I was not willing to confess Him. I tried not to deny Him, but I was not willing to declare Him innocent. I tried not to crucify Him, but I was not willing to crown Him Lord of my life. What did I know, compared to what you know?

You have the New Testament. I was not aware of the meaning of this. You have seen His resurrection. You know that He is the glorious Son of God. You have heard the Good News of the Gospel—the free gift of forgiveness and eternal life, if you will trust in Him. I was not aware of all these things.

You know more than I. There are some of you who have taken

that middle ground for years. You have tried to sit on the fence. I urge you to not reject Him.

While there is time, crown Him Lord of all. Confess Him as your Savior. Receive Him as your Master or deny Him unto the Cross, as I did. There is no fence. There is no middle ground. I know because I am Pontius Pilate.

CHAPTER 10

BARABBAS[16]

Therefore, when they had gathered together, Pilate said to them, "Whom do you want me to release to you? Barabbas, or Jesus who is called Christ?"

MATTHEW 27:17

VOX POPULI, VOX DEI—the voice of the people is the voice of God. Or so the saying goes. But is it really true? Is it ever true? It has also been said that 50 million Frenchmen can't be wrong, but I wonder if 50 million Frenchmen, in theological matters, can ever be right. It is the *remnant* that shall be saved. Few there be that find the way to life, and many there are that go in to destruction, said Christ (Matthew 7:14). Is it not far more often the case *vox populi, vox diabolos*—the voice of the people is the voice of the devil?

Come with me that we may discover more. Let the leaves of the calendar of your mind flit back through the centuries until they come at last to that black Friday men call "Good."

In the midst of the tumultuous events of this fatal Friday morning, we discover a precious and scintillating jewel, a tiny vignette which, though small, is precious and contains within itself the very quintessence of the Christian faith.

I think it would be well to look again into that little vignette and see clearly what God would have us to understand during the passion season about what is, indeed, the real essence of Christianity. It involves a man who never in his wildest dreams ever thought he would become

107

a part of passion history, a part of redemption history—a man who suddenly appears out of nowhere and disappears into obscurity just as quickly.

I have searched the writings of the Church Fathers, the Anti-Nicene Fathers; I have searched dictionaries, encyclopedias, and commentaries and cannot find a word with any authenticity about what happened to this man after that morning. He appears on the world's stage for just a brief hour and then is gone. But he leaves for us a magnificent truth that every one of us should understand. His name: Barabbas.

If we are to understand the tremendous meaning of this tiny vignette, we are going to have to do a bit of biblical detective work. So if you are ready, put on your Sherlock Holmes cap, take your magnifying glass in hand, and come with me. Let us see what we might discover. We don't have many clues, but there are at least a few.

The first clue: his name. His name may tell us a good deal if we dissect it. Barabbas is an unusual name. What does it mean? The word *Ben*, in Hebrew, means "son" and is common enough. For example: *Ben-Hadad*, means "son of Hadad"; Ben-Jamin literally means "son of my right hand." But in Aramaic, the common language of the people of that day, the prefix *Ben* is changed to *Bar.*

Let us consider the meaning of the name Barabbas. What does Abbas mean? Does that sound familiar? Isn't that the word Paul uses in Romans 8? You are absolutely correct. You see, it's elementary, my dear Watson. Paul said, "For you did not receive the spirit of bondage again to fear; but you received the Spirit of adoption by whom we cry out, 'Abba, Father'" (Romans 8:15). So that's it. It means "father."

Well, yes, it does—but not quite. The word for "father" in Hebrew is *av*, but Abba, they say, is a diminutive form, a term of endearment. We might not be far afield if we said that it meant *daddy*. So Barabbas was the "son of a father," the beloved son of a father, who apparently grew up to break his daddy's heart.

As a second clue, we can discover something about his politics.

That may tell us a good bit about a man. We see that Barabbas was an insurrectionist, a Zealot. The Zealots were the revolutionary party in Israel. They not only hated Rome, but determined to do something about it. They were determined to throw off the heavy yoke of Rome. Barabbas was one of the Zealots, and though many of them began with high ideals, unfortunately, as so often is the case, many of them gradually degenerated until they became mere brigands—highwaymen, cutthroats, robbers, and murderers. Barabbas was numbered among these Zealots.

We might remember that though the Zealots hated the Romans with an intense hatred, there was another group they hated even more: the Publicans—those turncoat Jews who collected taxes from their own people and turned them over to the Roman overlords. They hated these people with a fiery hatred. Perhaps you never realized how astonishing it is that within the tiny band of the twelve disciples, there was another Zealot. It was Simon. Not Simon Bar Jonah (Peter), but Simon the Zealot—Simon Zelotes, he is called.

Wonder of wonders, also in that same tiny band we find a tax collector—a publican. His name was Levi. We know him more familiarly as Matthew, who authored one of the Gospels. A tax collector and a Zealot, together, intimately for three and a half years. Only the incredible influence of the grace and love of Christ kept the dagger of Simon Zelotes out of the heart of Levi, the tax collector.

But our Zealot, Barabbas, had no such mollifying influences upon his own life. He descended from bad to worse, until he became nothing better than a cutthroat, a murderer, and a robber. There came a day when he found himself surrounded by the glitter of Roman spears. He was captured, his hands tied, and he was bundled off to prison. There, at Pilate's praetorian, there upon the Gabbatha (the place of trial), he was peremptorily tried and just as peremptorily condemned to Roman justice, which meant the cross.

So on this day, far below the praetorian, in a dungeon deep in the darkness of that palace, sits Barabbas, with several other Zealot companions, waiting for their execution. Already they can feel the nails piercing their flesh, and the agony of the cross.

It is about six o'clock in the morning. The sun has only barely risen above the horizon and begun to peek over the distant hills. Only the very pinnacle of the temple can be seen, whereas the Dead Sea still lies enshrouded in darkness and mystery below. But though the city still is covered with darkness, there is a sound of men afoot, the shuffle of sandals on the cobblestones, soft knocking at doors, and whispered voices: "They've taken Him. They've captured Jesus. The Sanhedrin has condemned Him to die. Come, they've brought Him to Pilate. Let's see Him today. This may be the day when he reveals His mighty power and throws off the yoke of Rome."

So it began. At first just a trickle, then a stream, and then a great river of humanity pours forth from the city, as they made their way to the Pavement, to Gabbatha, the palace of Pilate. Meanwhile, inside, the procurator of Judea, Pontius Pilate, was still asleep on his couch. It fell to his guard to awaken him. He said, "Sire, the High Priests are outside. In fact, the entire Sanhedrin seems to be here. They have a bound prisoner with them, and they are demanding that you try Him now."

"Now, you say? In the middle of the night they want me to try Him?"

"Well, sire, it is six o'clock in the morning."

Pilate got up out of his bed, dressed, and went out to the Pavement and sat down upon his imperial throne chair, from which he meted out justice, Roman style. He didn't appreciate being dragged out of bed to settle what seemed to him to be an intramural conflict among the Jews. They have their own law; let them sort out the pieces. But the temple authorities were determined to put Him to death.

As we saw earlier, Pilate figured he could appease the enemies of Jesus by giving Him over to scourging, not realizing that by doing this, he was helping to fulfill the words of Isaiah the prophet, written 700 years before that day. As the Scripture says:

I gave My back to those who struck Me,

And My cheeks to those who plucked out the beard;

I did not hide My face from shame and spitting (Isaiah 50:6).

The cruel scourges of the Roman soldiers plowed their way across His back until there was not a spot on his body, from His neck to His ankles that wasn't turned into an open wound. Then, covered with a mocking robe of purple, a crown of thorns on His brow, and a broken reed in His hand, they led Him back out to the Pavement.

Pilate looked at Him and was shocked. Even his hard heart was stunned as he saw the bloodstained purple robe, and he saw the agony this man had been through. He said to the crowd, "Behold, the man!"

The people, to his astonishment, said, "Away with this man. Away with this man! Let Him be crucified." Pilate could not believe his ears. They were like wild dogs that had their teeth in flesh and weren't going to let go until they consumed it.

Then Pilate hit on another expedient. "Ah, yes, it is our custom on the Passover to set a prisoner free." No doubt a remnant, historians say, from the original Passover when the Jews were delivered out of the bondage of Egypt. Pilate said to himself, "I will set before them the most miserable, wretched prisoner we have and let them choose. Surely they will take this prophet rather than the most wicked criminal we can come up with. Whom shall I call for? Let's see. Ah . . . ah yes, that fellow, that brigand I condemned just last week. What was his name? His name . . . His name, ah . . . Barabbas. That's what it was, Barabbas. Centurion. Bring up Barabbas."

So, a cohort of soldiers descends flight after flight of stone stairs, down into the dungeon below. They open the iron door on creaking hinges, letting the light in, blinding the eyes of those who had dwelt in darkness. With laughter in his voice, the soldier says, "Well, now my chickadees, rise and shine. It's a lovely day outside, and we have prepared for you a little picnic on a hill outside the city wall. Oh yes, you, Barabbas, the governor wants to see you upstairs."

Barabbas stumbles out into the bright sunlight, shading his eyes against the glare. He finds himself standing before a great mob, swaying back and forth. Once, they were individuals. But now they have turned into a hydra-headed monster thirsting for the blood of this strange prophet who stands next to him, dripping His own blood.

Pilate looks at both of them. Then he gives the crowd a choice—the innocent Man or the murderer. Which should be released: Barabbas or Jesus?

They cried out, "Barabbas! Barabbas! Release to us Barabbas!"

Pilate exclaimed, "Why? What evil has He done? What shall I do then with this Jesus which is called Christ?"

The people cried out with one voice, "Let Him be crucified! Crucify this one! Let Him be crucified!"

Pilate, of course, relented. He went through the charade of washing his hands as if that would exonerate him from the responsibility of handing Jesus over to be crucified.

The guards led Jesus, bearing His Cross, down the Via Dolorosa to the hill of Golgotha, that bleak, bloodstained and lonely hill—the place of death. There they crucified Him.

Barabbas was free. You would think he would run out of Jerusalem as fast as he could, but he could not leave. He had to see what was happening. He made his way down the Via Dolorosa to the Place of the Skull—to Golgotha. Not only was Jesus there, but also there were two thieves—presumably acquaintances of Barabbas. One was on His right, and one on His left. One could picture Barabbas as he takes this scene in:

> I recognized them. They had been in the prison the night before. All of us condemned criminals were there together. Two of them were hanging on crosses, but the middle cross should have been mine. It was occupied by this Jesus. I went closer—I just could not help myself. I heard the insults and the mockery people were hurling at him.

Even one of my two buddies was part of it. Then I heard the other thief speak, rebuking the first.

"Don't you fear God," he said, "since you are under the same sentence? We are punished justly, for we are getting what our deeds deserve. But this man has done nothing wrong." Then he said, "Jesus, remember me when you come into Your kingdom."

Jesus answered him, "I tell you the truth, today you will be with Me in paradise" (Luke 23:40-43 NIV).

I couldn't believe it. Jesus just handed a dying criminal a type of absolution. He was dying too, but obviously He was no criminal. At that moment, I knew that what my fellow criminal had just received was even better and far more valuable than my own gift of freedom. I wanted more than anything to hear those words being spoken to me, "Today you will be with Me in paradise."

Barabbas was no theologian. He, perhaps, knew nothing about redemption or substitutionary atonement. But there was one thing he knew down to the very core of his being: *That Man was dying in his place.* That was *his* Cross; those were his spikes, that was his death He was dying there on that Cross. Barabbas knew the meaning of Calvary.

For *you* are Barabbas and *I* am Barabbas. We are all Barabbas— sinful sons of sinful fathers.

Just like Barabbas, Jesus Christ died in our places, so we don't have to. He went to Hell for us, so we need never go. Will eternity be long enough to thank Him for what He has done for us? I wonder if Barabbas spent the rest of his life thanking God for dying in his place. Meanwhile, surely that is the way we should spend the rest of our lives.

"ALL THIS I DID FOR THEE; WHAT HAST THOU DONE FOR ME?"

When co-author Jerry Newcombe saw a preview of Mel Gibson's *The Passion of The Christ*, the first thing that leapt to his mind was the statement that helped give birth to one of the early Protestant missionary movements—that of Count von Zinzendorf (1700-1760). After an Easter service one year, the great Count von Zinzendorf, one of the wealthiest men in Europe at the time, noticed a huge painting of Christ at Calvary on the side wall of the church narthex. On a brass plate at the bottom of the painting were inscribed these words: "All this I did for thee; what hast thou done for Me?"

He stood there for long minutes just staring at the picture and reading again and again the inscription. The moments turned into hours and the day passed; it wasn't until the sun was already "westering," and the rays were coming in slantedly through the windows, that Zinzendorf knelt there with his heart melted by the love of Christ and brokenheartedly invited Him in. He turned over His vast estate to the Moravian Church for their missions headquarters, and through His wealth, missionaries have traveled all over the world.

When we contemplate how Jesus died in our place, just as He died in the place of Barabbas, may we remember the question that so moved Zinzendorf: "All this I did for thee; what hast thou done for Me?"

CHAPTER *11*

"I AM LONGINUS"

*So when the centurion, who stood opposite Him, saw
that He cried out like this and breathed His last, he said,
"Truly this Man was the Son of God!"*

MARK 15:39

TODAY YOU ARE GOING TO have a guided tour through the Holy of
Holies, and there is no one more qualified to lead that tour than I am.
No, I am not the high priest. In fact, I am not even a Jew; I am a Gen-
tile, and yet, there is no one more qualified than I. For you see, I was
there. I was there for all of it. I saw it happen. In fact, I made it happen.

My name is Longinus, and I am a Roman centurion. Oh, I know
your epithets—roughhewn, coarse, pitiless, merciless, but do you know
what it means to be a Roman centurion? You don't recognize me, but
if you had lived in my day, you would have. You would have known at
first glance that I was a Roman centurion. Whether it was that brightly
plumed legionnaire's helmet, the erect bearing, the white tunic, the
bronzed and burnished cuirass (breastplate), the Roman sword at one
side, the coiled whip on the other, the spear held at attention. Oh,
everyone in that day recognized a Roman centurion.

Do you know what it means to be part of the army of Rome? Yes,
I have found something out about your times, and I understand that for
decades you have been one of the world's two superpowers. Ah, what
is that to a Roman? For the last decade or so, you claimed to be the
only superpower for a whole dozen years. Do you not know that Rome
was the only superpower in the world for *seven hundred years,* and

during all of that time, the Roman army scarcely lost a battle? That is what it means to be a Roman centurion.

If you had looked into my face, you would have seen carved there the image of Caesar. Caesar's army was invincible. If you had looked into my steel-gray eyes, you would have seen death march across the plain. You could have almost heard the stomp of boots, the clash of swords and spears, and the anguished cries of the dying and the wounded. My business was death, and I was a master of my trade.

A LIFE-CHANGING ASSIGNMENT

I was assigned to deal with these cantankerous Jews, who were always rising up and rebelling. I had the task of protecting the governor and his household. Therefore, it fell to me to be the one standing guard on that fatal morning when the sun had not yet risen in the sky over the mountains, but the brightness cast strange, eerie purple shadows on the white columns of the temple.

There was the sound of a tumult outside. At first I thought it was but the changing of the guard; I was just coming on duty at six o'clock in the morning. I immediately rushed out to see what the commotion was. To my amazement, there stood virtually the entire Sanhedrin and the high priest with a prisoner whose hands were bound in front of Him. They were demanding that Pilate immediately try this prisoner before the bar of Roman justice. Well, at least they knew that it was to us they must come for justice.

It was my onerous task to arouse Pilate from his couch. As you can well imagine, he was not overly thrilled to be awakened at that hour of the morning, but he quickly dressed and came out. He sat down and looked over this mob before him. Pilate asked them, "What accusation do you bring against this Man?" They went back and forth, until his ears perked up at learning that the accused was a Galilean, at which point he gladly sent Jesus to Herod. That was that. Pontius Pilate was through with the matter and could return to sleep.

If only that had been the end of the matter.

When they brought Jesus back to Pilate, they hurled more accusations against Him, but the accused did not even defend Himself.

Once again, Pilate, hearing more accusations thrown against Jesus, brought Him into the palace. I heard the conversation, for I was there. Pilate said, "Do you not hear how many things they testify against You? What have you done?" (Matthew 27:13, John 18:35b).

Jesus answered him never a word. I marveled at His silence, for all the prisoners I had ever seen brought before the governor would instantly fall upon their knees and begin to snivel and plead for mercy and beg for deliverance from their tormentors. This man said nothing. Even Pilate was astonished to the point of irritation. "Are you not speaking to me? Do you not know that I have power to crucify You, and power to release You?" (John 19:10).

Then Jesus said the most astonishing thing. He almost seemed to rebuke the governor. He said to him: "You could have no power at all against Me unless it had been given you from above. Therefore the one who delivered Me to you has the greater sin" (John 19:11).

From that moment, Pilate seemed to want to let this man go. He brought Him out again and said, "I have examined Him and have found no fault in this Man regarding these accusations you bring against Him. Nor has Herod. . . .Therefore. . . ."

That's right, Pilate, tell them now. Tell them who is in charge here. You are the Roman governor. You have all the power of Rome. Not only the Jerusalem garrison is here, but also all of the troops are up from Caesarea for this feast, lest there be an uprising among the people. You have more than enough people to put down an uprising here, Pilate. Tell them who is in charge.

"I will therefore scourge him."

What? Scourge Him? You just said He had done nothing amiss. Of course, it was not my place to challenge orders. I was to obey. That was my whole life—obeying orders. So we led Jesus into the back courtyard, and there He was stripped of His robes and tied to a column. I appointed two of my burliest guards the task of scourging. A Roman scourge, my friend, would send a chill down anyone's back. The short-handled whips were made of three long pieces of rawhide with sharp sheep bones imbedded in the end of each. This was no flailing. Upon contact, these bones would bite into the skin and oftentimes tear a rib right out of the rib cage.

SCOURGING

I thought, "This man has held His peace until now, but here, He, like all of the rest, will find His voice." The first guard brought the whip back. I heard it whistle through the air and then the crack as it contacted the skin. There was an instant inhaling of air . . . but the cursing never came. I thought to myself, "Perhaps it will take two blows of the whip for Him to find His voice." Again, the whip came down . . . and again. The crack was heard throughout the courtyard, over and over and over and over again, until finally there wasn't a part of His body that wasn't bloody, dripping red.

At last I gave the order to cut Him down. He collapsed onto the pavement, but our soldiers were ready for that as well. They took a bucket filled with vinegar water and splashed it on His back. This brought Him instantly back to consciousness. Then my soldiers decided to enjoy themselves, because they despised these people, who often fell upon them at night—these zealots with their knives, who had cut the throats of many of their cohorts. They found a filthy old purple robe and put it on His bloody back. They placed a reed in His hand and pressed a crown of thorns on His brow—then bowed the knee and said, mockingly, "Hail, king of the Jews."

When the taunts had gone on long enough, I brought Him back to Pilate, who, when he looked at Him, would be sure it would satisfy the blood lust even of these people. He led Him out again to the top of the Pavement. He looked down at the mob and said, "Behold, the Man." Surely, this would suffice, thought Pilate.

But you know how it turned out. The mob demanded that they crucify Him. They wouldn't shut up.

I knew that Pilate would bend, but he certainly would not give in completely to this rabble. To my utter astonishment, he called for a basin of water and a towel and ceremoniously dipped his hands in the water, washed them, and said, "I am innocent of the blood of this just Person. You see to it" (Matthew 27:24b), and he gave Him into their hands. I could not believe it. What has happened to Roman law and justice that an innocent man should be crucified?

However, it was not my job to disobey, so we prepared the crosses for Him and two other prisoners. We made our way down what you call the Via Dolorosa, turning this way and that. As I rode before them on my horse, I could look back and see the trail of blood running down His legs and dripping from His feet. Finally, His strength was gone altogether, and He collapsed beneath the heavy load of the Cross, just as we reached the city gate. I saw a man coming in the gate, and I hailed him and commanded him to take up the load. They helped Jesus to His feet and prodded Him upward, up the hill Golgotha, that blackened hill, that place of the skull, the place of death where so many thousands had been crucified before. Golgotha was right outside the city gate, right by the highway where all of the Jews could see what happened to those who broke the laws of Rome.

GOLGOTHA

The other two prisoners were securely fixed. In the midst of their curses and screams, we threw this man to His back on top of the Cross, with one legionnaire on each foot and arm. I placed my knee upon His right forearm and took one of the spikes out of my belt. With a heavy iron hammer, I prepared to pound it into the base of His hand.

I looked at His face—which always before was turned the other way, with the eyes tightly closed—expecting to see a look of absolute pain and horror. To my astonishment, His eyes were open. He was looking right into my face with a look that I swear to the gods was a look of compassion—a look of love—which I could not understand. I tore my gaze away. Duty beckoned me, and I placed the spike at the heel of His hand. With one powerful blow, I drove it into the wood of the crossbeam. The same was done to the left hand and then to the feet. One foot was crossed on top of the other, raising the feet some eight inches to continue the pain longer than would take place if they were stretched out (otherwise asphyxiation would kill the prisoner in a few moments.) He would now linger for hours—possibly even days.

The soldiers picked up the Cross. I knew the absolute length, the farthest extent of any man's endurance would come. I had seen courage, but not like this. When they dropped that Cross into a cubit-deep hole in the ground, I was sure the rending of flesh, the ripping of ligaments would bring the most blood-curdling scream from His lips, as it did from everyone else. But when that Cross dropped heavily into the ground, there was again the inhalation of breath . . . and nothing. I looked up in amazement. Why wasn't He cursing me?

I saw Him looking down at me again. Then He lifted His eyes up to Heaven and said the most amazing thing I had ever heard in my life. He said, "Father, forgive them for they do not know what they do" (Luke 23:34). The heavy hammer fell from my hand with a thud upon the rocky hill. I had seen hatred in battle, I had seen determination unto death. I had seen courage in the raw, but I had never in my life ever seen anyone pray for those who were killing him.

I staggered back from the Cross too amazed hardly even able to think or to speak. Finally, I turned my back to this One that I could look on no longer and joined my cohorts, who were gambling for His garments. Slowly, interminably, the moments, the minutes, the hours passed by. The priests and elders came and mocked Him and laughed at Him, and even one of those crucified with Him railed against Him.

Then something phenomenal happened at noon. In the midst of a clear sky, suddenly, the sun began to grow dark. I thought that surely a thick cloud had covered the sun, but I looked up and saw that the sky was clear. It got darker and darker. One of my soldiers said, "Centurion, is it an eclipse?"

I said, "You dolt, there's a full moon. There can be no eclipse of the sun in a full moon. Don't you know anything at all?"

"Then what is it, centurion?"

I said, "How should I know? I've never seen anything like it before." There was an eeriness about the darkness. People stood in awe. They gradually backed away from the crosses and a silence spread over that place of the skull. There was no sound except a soft wind blowing past the crosses and the slow dripping of blood into the pools formed below.

At three o'clock in the afternoon, suddenly the silence was torn in two by a cry that seemed to rise up right out of the pit of Hell. "*Eloi, Eloi, lama sabachthani?*" I have since learned that that's Aramaic—the native tongue of Jesus—for "My God, My God, why have You forsaken Me?" Though I did not understand, I heard someone say that He cried for Elijah, and another said, "Well, let's see if Elijah will come and take Him down."

He cried again with a loud voice, "It is finished." It was not the voice of a dying man; it was the voice of a conqueror. "*Tetelestai*"— that is to say, "It is done. It is paid. It is accomplished." With that, His head fell onto His breast as He gave up the ghost.

LONGINUS' CONFESSION

My mouth was hanging open when I saw Him thus—crying aloud and then giving up the ghost. Suddenly there was a tremor in the ground, and I said, "Truly, this was a righteous man." That tremor changed into a positive shaking—an earthquake. Boulders began to split, fall, and roll down the hill. People were thrown to the ground onto their faces and backs. The women were screaming. There was drawn forth out of my heart and my mind the cry, "Truly, this man was the Son of God."

Yes, I said those very words. I, who was the one who took a spear and with that Roman lance pierced His side, and to the astonishment of all, there came out blood and water. I, who as your Scriptures say, pierced the veil of His flesh that opened up the Holy of Holies.

Yes, I was there in that holiest place. If you have read your history, you know that cry of mine was not in vain—that I came to understand, indeed, that this was the Son of God and that He had died in my place, for my sins, and I embraced Him as my own Savior and Lord.

I came to understand later that it was sin that put Him on that Cross. It was your sins, as well as mine, that brought Him to that accursed tree and to that agony. He was dying for our transgressions. It was our lies, our lusts, our pride, our greed, our hate—all of these things that raked His body and drew His blood and pierced His heart. I was forgiven for what I did, and that was the purpose. He died so that we might be forgiven.

CHAPTER 12

"I AM THOMAS"

Then He said to Thomas, "Reach your finger here, and look at My hands; and reach your hand here, and put it into My side. Do not be unbelieving, but believing." And Thomas answered and said to Him, "My Lord and my God!"

JOHN 20:27-28

I SUPPOSE THAT SOME OF YOU think that it is easy to be a minister of Jesus Christ, to always do the right thing at the right time, to live in a glass house, to say the right thing, to think the right thing, to believe the right thing. Let me assure you, my friend, it is not.

There is something that I believe I need to get straight today.

Actually, I have heard some comments, some rumors. I have heard it said, "Well, he slipped; he has actually deviated from the faith." I believe the word "apostatized" has been used. Some have said that I have actually denied the resurrection of Jesus Christ.

As loath as I am to bring this up, I believe it is something that must be dealt with. My name has spread far and wide to many lands, and now that rumor is spreading with it. Therefore, I think it must be dealt with frankly and honestly. I know that you say you have evidence; you say that in front of a group of notable ministers I actually said that Jesus Christ did not rise from the dead. Well, did I or didn't I?

As shocking as it may be to some of you, I think I would have to be perfectly honest and say that I *did* make that statement. Furthermore, I meant it. I told them that dead men don't walk or talk again;

that it was impossible; it was contrary to all the laws of nature. Regardless of what they said, it just was a scientific impossibility and one that I could not believe.

I know that some of you are gathering your pharisaical robes around you, picking up stones to hurl, but before you cast the first one, I think there are some things you should know. First, I, indeed, followed Him—followed Him more than most, I would say. For years I followed Him, and I did it sincerely; I did it with all of my heart, and I can honestly say that I loved Him. I was never ashamed to say that. In fact, I even gave up my job for Him.

There were times when I didn't know where my next meal was coming from or where I would lay my head. There were times when my life was in jeopardy because of Him, but I followed Him. I remember that day when my life was changed. He had gathered some of His disciples around Him. I remember He looked me straight in the face and said to me, "Thomas, follow Me." From that day forward, my soul was conscripted by this Man, and I went wherever He would have me to go. I loved Him and I believed in Him.

For some of you who really don't know me at all, I should, perhaps, introduce myself more fully. My name is Thomas. But my first name is most emphatically not "Doubting," as some of you are so frequently wont to say. In fact, there are some of you who can't even mention my name without adding that cursed appellation, "Doubting"—"*Doubting* Thomas."

But what do you know about it? What do you know about what it really was like having your life on the line every day for Him, not knowing whether you are going to live to see another morning or not?

You say I am a coward. Is that a fact? Perhaps you have forgotten that time when we had gone across Jordan, and the Sanhedrin's trap was closing upon us. We all knew that the days were numbered. It was while we were there that we received the message that Lazarus was sick. Jesus waited two days, and then He said, "We go to Bethany." You should have heard some of your brave apostles then, as I heard them. "Bethany? Why, that's but a stone's throw from Jerusalem. We will be captured. They will kill us. We will all be crucified. We can't go to Bethany."

That is what Peter and John and the rest of them said. But it was I, "Doubting Thomas," as you so facilely say, who stood up and said, "Let us also go [with Him to Bethany], that we may die with Him" (John 11:16). It was I who led that expedition to the very borders of Jerusalem. It was I who placed our lives on the line. It was I, "Doubting Thomas."

After being in Bethany, we went back to Jerusalem. I had had such hopes, such dreams that this was He who would redeem Israel and cast off the yoke of Rome. I should have known better. All of my other dreams and aspirations had crumbled into dust. Why should I have thought it would be different with this one? Indeed, within a short space of twenty-four hours, we saw this One who had stilled the sea and calmed the storm taken by rough hands, bound, led away, and then condemned, convicted, scourged, and crucified.

At some distance I watched, hour after hour, interminably, until at last His head slumped onto His chest, the slow dripping of blood into pools there on that barren rocky hill ceased, and He was dead. My hopes were dead. My dreams were dead, my aspirations were dead, and my soul was dead within me. All I had hoped for was gone, and now it seemed that a heavy black pall hung over my life.

I managed somehow to make it through the days and the nights, though my sleep was frequently interrupted by the ringing of the hammer on those spikes. How many times have I been startled awake by that sound—a sound I am sure I shall hear until the day I die. That picture of those three crosses athwart the sky is indelibly etched in my memory. But He was dead.

I helped to take Him down from the Cross. Have you ever handled dead flesh, felt the icy cold stiffened limbs, and tried to close those unseeing eyes? I helped carry Him to the tomb. Yes, I saw it, I felt it, and if there is one thing I knew above anything else in this world, I knew that *He was dead.*

But it was about the third night afterward, as I was dragging myself to my bed, hoping the ringing of those hammers would not waken me again from my sleep, when suddenly there came an excited pounding on my door. I said, "Hold on, hold on, I'll be there." I opened the door, and to my amazement, there stood the whole bunch of them—all of His disciples. They were shouting and talking and waving their arms. I couldn't make heads or tails of what they were saying. I said, "Wait a minute, one at a time. What are you saying?"

Then I heard the words, "He's alive. The Lord is alive. He's alive!"

I said, "Just . . . one . . . minute. He is not alive. He is dead. I saw Him. I touched Him. He is dead! I put Him in a tomb."

They kept prattling on about the fact that they had seen Him. I thought, "These poor people, so eager to have that relationship continue, have deceived themselves into imagining that He is alive still." I finally dismissed them with these words: "He is dead." When they insisted again that He was alive, I said to them, "I do not believe it," and "Unless I see in His hands the print of the nails, and put my finger into the print of the nails, and put my hand into His side, I will not believe" (John 20:25). "Get out of here and let me sleep."

Yes, they were a noted group of apostles, all right, and I did deny that He was alive—I admit that freely. I was as convinced as anything I have ever been convinced of in this world. But to my utter astonishment, the next day, when I went out into the streets of Jerusalem, I was amazed to hear this rumor being spread abroad everywhere. People were whispering, "He's alive. Did you hear? Jesus is alive. He's alive. He's risen from the dead."

Then I was gripped with fear. Perhaps that was the reason I agreed to meet with them the following Sunday night. Perhaps I could at least straighten these people out before they got themselves killed. I felt I owed them at least that. There in the same Upper Room again, though the doors were locked for fear of the authorities, I said to them, "Get this straight. He is not alive. He is dead. I know that He is dead. Give this up. Do you realize this is not only a foolish fantasy you are entertaining, but this is fatally dangerous? You are all going to get yourselves nailed to a cross, like He was."

They treated me as if I were some sort of retarded child who just didn't understand—some benighted heathen who needed to be enlightened. They smiled condescendingly at me and shook their heads. That just made me all the more furious, until finally, I turned my plate away from them and finished the meal. I turned my thoughts inward, while they continued chattering about this insanity of His being alive.

I was taken up in a reverie. There was something about that room that drew my thoughts back ten days before, when we had met together in this same room. Only then He *was* alive; then He was with us. I remembered the magic of His presence and the music of His voice. There was something electric about it. I could hear Him again in my mind, as clearly as when He spoke it, "In My Father's house are many mansions; if it were not so, I would have told you. I go to prepare a place for you. And if I go and prepare a place for you, I will come again and receive you to Myself . . ." (John 14:2-3).

I thought, "What did that mean?"

He went on, "And where I go you know, and the way you know" (v. 4).

It was I who said to Him, "Lord, we do not know where You are going, and how can we know the way?" (v. 5).

It was to me, Thomas, that He said the following words you love to repeat so often, though you have probably forgotten to whom He said them. He said, "I am the way, the truth, and the life. No one comes to the Father except through Me" (v. 6). Those enigmatic sayings of His were so hard to understand. What did He mean? We couldn't understand—none of us knew what He was talking about.

Suddenly I was jerked out of this reverie by the startling realization that the chattering had ceased; the room had grown suddenly silent, and an eerie quiet hung over it. I lifted my head, and I looked into the faces of Peter, John, Matthew, Bartholomew, and Philip . . . they were all staring at me. What had I done?

Suddenly, I realized they weren't looking at me. They were looking past me—over my left shoulder, toward the back of the room where the door was locked. There was something that seemed to be irresistibly pulling me to turn and look. I was actually afraid of what I might see, but I could withhold myself no longer. Slowly I turned and there . . . there in the shadows, just beyond the light cast by the candles on the table, stood a figure in a white robe. Could it be? Is it . . . Is it He? Of course not. It is not He. He is dead.

Then there came a voice, "Peace to you." Suddenly I realized it must be some cruel impersonation, some sick joke—no doubt for my sake entirely. I stood suddenly to my feet, causing the dishes on the table to rattle. I was about to tell them what I thought of their sick humor and stomp out of the room, when all of a sudden He stepped out of the shadows and into the light, and I saw His face. It was *Jesus*! It was He. It was He. It can't be. He's dead. I saw Him.

He's alive. But dead men don't walk, and yet He was walking straight toward me. As He approached, He extended His hands before Him, and I looked right through those gaping holes. He said to me, "Reach your finger here, and look at My hands; and reach your hand here, and put it into My side" (John 20:27).

He had heard what I said. He had heard that I denied Him. He had heard my words. My knees grew weak. My whole body was limp. I collapsed onto my knees in front of Him and found myself staring into those mangled feet. My eyes were drawn irresistibly up, and I looked into a face of compassion and love itself. There was suddenly wrung from my soul this confession, "My Lord and my God" (v. 28).

In that instant, as if some mighty wind had blown the cobwebs out of my mind, my doubts disappeared and I *believed*. My heart was filled with such joy; it seemed like a burning of fire that cleansed my body of all of my sin, and I, indeed, believed. In fact, Jesus Himself confirmed that fact. He said, "Thomas . . . you have believed . . ." (v. 29).

"Doubting Thomas," indeed. "Doubting Thomas"? Doubtless Thomas is my name, for I have that confirmed by Christ, the Master Himself, and don't you ever forget it. I couldn't contain myself. I was suddenly one of them. I was filled with that same excitement and joy. I wanted to tell everyone, "He's alive. He's alive from the dead! Death isn't the end. We will not die, but will live forever."

I told my friends and my relatives and everyone I saw. That faith took me all the way to India. Why is it that Thomas is so popular a name in that country? Because it was I who established that Church. It was I who proclaimed that the Son of God has come and died and risen from the dead. For in the very moment that I believed, suddenly I saw it all so clearly—I understood. "Oh, Thomas," I said, "you fool." For I remembered that I had said, "Let us go and die with Him." I could not die with Him. He came to die for me, in my place, that I might not have to die, that I might live forever.

"I am the way, the truth and the life. I go to prepare a place for you," He had said. I did not realize what He meant, but now I knew. He went to that black and lonely hill, and there He paid for a place for me in Paradise. He was offering it freely to me and to all those who would trust in Him, and I, having trusted, received that assurance that I had eternal life.

Ah, dear friend, I am convinced that I am not and I was not so different from you. What is it that you seek? What is it that you want? Is it not certainty, some evidence, some proof of the reality of life after death, a heart-to-heart, face-to-face, soul-to-soul encounter that will cause you to know that you shall live forever?

It was that assurance that took me through many lands where they had no clue of this great news. I went east telling everyone along the way, through Persia—what you now call Iran—all the way to India, even the southernmost tip. This filled my life with the excitement and joy of proclaiming the glorious resurrection of Jesus Christ.

There came a day when the heathen captured me and condemned me as well. They bound my hands as His were bound. Then I saw the executioner coming with his huge curved sword, and I saw those strong hands and those large arms. But do you know what? They didn't frighten me at all, because when I looked at his hands, I saw the holes in the hands of Jesus as well, and I remembered that day, that night when I had seen Him alive from the dead, and I said, "Executioner, do your worst. You cannot kill me, for I shall live again. I fear you not." On that day, the headsman's blade flashed in the Asian sun and I put on immortality.

I did not die. I have never died. As Jesus said, "Whoever lives and believes in Me shall never die" (John 11:26). Even my body shall be raised to walk again upon the earth.

If you would like to have that peace, that assurance, that certainty of life eternal, then I urge you to look up as I did into His compassionate, loving face. Having seen the nail prints in His hands and feet and now knowing that He endured all of this for us, if you can say to Him as I said, from the very depth of your heart: "My Lord and my God." In that moment you, too, can have that assurance, and you will doubtless come to be a "Doubtless Thomas" just like me.

PART IV

THE POWER
AND PROMISE
OF THE PASSION

CHAPTER *13*

HE IS RISEN INDEED

If in this life only we have hope in Christ,
we are of all men the most pitiable.

1 CORINTHIANS 15:19

THE POWER OF THE PASSION of Jesus Christ is seen most clearly in His triumph over the grave.

The evidence for the bodily resurrection of Christ is overwhelming. That is to say, the evidence is overwhelming—unless you reject the miraculous *a priori* before you study the facts. However, that is not a very objective way to approach anything. Christianity is based on a deep foundation, a foundation that cannot be shaken despite all the attacks against it. The single most important event in Christianity is the resurrection of Christ.

Dr. Thomas Arnold, nineteenth century professor of history at Oxford and the author of *History of Rome*, once said:

> I have been used for many years to study the histories of other times, and to examine and weigh the evidence of those who have written about them, and I know of no one fact in the history of mankind which is proved by better and fuller evidence of every sort, to the understanding of a fair inquirer than the great sign which God hath given us that Christ died and rose again from the dead.[17]

THE CORNERSTONE OF THE CHRISTIAN FAITH

The evidence for the bodily resurrection of Jesus is compelling. It is an indisputable fact that the disciples of Jesus were emboldened and transformed from scared rabbits into courageous and bold witnesses who could not be hushed up. The Resurrection is so critically important because it is the cornerstone of the Christian faith. Take away the Resurrection and Christianity crumbles like a house of cards. Some of the liberal denominations have taken it away from their statements of faith, and their churches are withering away—for their congregations instinctively know that there is nothing there but froth, and they will not tolerate being deceived. If Christ were not bodily raised from the dead in human history, Christianity would cease to exist.

The historical, bodily resurrection of Christ from the dead is unique among world religions. Confucius died and was buried. Lao-tse wandered off and died with his water buffalo. Buddha rotted with food poisoning. Mohammed died in 632, and his body was cut up and spread all over the near East. But Jesus rose from the dead. By that Resurrection from the dead, He demonstrated that He was indeed the Son of God with power. By His life, by His death, by His resurrection, He declares that He is God. Let's examine the case for the resurrection of Christ.

THE RELEVANT EVIDENCE

Any case must deal with all of the relevant evidence. Therefore, when we are dealing with the resurrection of Christ, we need to look at all the evidence.

It says in Acts that Christ "presented Himself alive after His suffering by many infallible proofs" (Acts 1:3). I want to examine seven pieces of evidence and seven theories that attempt to explain them away.

SEVEN PIECES OF EVIDENCE

First, there is the Christian Church, which is the largest institution or organization that has ever existed on the face of the earth, with membership easily passing two billion people. Nothing comparable to her or even close has ever existed before. The Grand Canyon wasn't caused by an Indian dragging a stick, and the Christian Church wasn't created by a myth.

Historians—secular unbelieving historians—tell us that the Christian Church began in Jerusalem in 30 A.D., the year Christ was killed, and that she began because the apostles began to preach that Jesus Christ rose from the dead. You strip everything else away from their preaching, and their main message was the death and resurrection of Christ (e.g., Acts 2:23-24).

Second, there is the empty tomb. Again, many adherents to many religions can travel to the place where the founder of their religion is currently entombed and say, "Here lies the dust of our estimable founder." You cannot say that about Christ. He is not in the grave. He is risen.

For 1,700 years there was virtually no controversy that the tomb was empty. The Jews didn't deny it. The Romans didn't deny it. Nobody denied it until just recently. With our vast "rear-view mirror" wisdom, we look back through more than 1,900 years and we decide, "Oh, the tomb wasn't empty." Too bad those who were there couldn't have been so smart.

Third, there is the Roman seal. The huge rock had a rope stretched across it; clay was fastened to the rope and to the wall of the tomb, and the Roman seal was impressed upon it. If you broke that, you broke the seal. If you broke the seal, you "incurred the wrath of Roman law."[18] The penalty was death.

Fourth, there was the Roman guard. According to Professor Harold Smith, "A Watch usually consisted of four men, each of whom watched in turn, while the others rested beside him so as to be roused by the least alarm. However, in this case the guard may have been more numerous."[19] These Roman soldiers were well trained. These people were experts in what they did. The penalty for leaving their post or for falling asleep at the job was death[20]—a penalty that was "always rigorously enforced."[21]

Fifth, there was the stone—which weighed at least two tons—

probably more. The opening would indicate that the stone would have to be at least about seven or eight feet high. It took more than one person to move it.

Sixth, there were Christ's post-resurrection appearances. These are crucial. He appeared to one, then to another, then to two, then to three and then to eight, ten, eleven and five hundred people at a time, over a period of about six weeks (1 Corinthians 15:4-9). They saw Him, they heard Him, and they handled Him. He fixed breakfast for them. He ate fish with them (John 21:7-15; Luke 24:42-43).

Connected to the appearances is the transformation of the apostles. One day they were cringing in an upper room for fear of the Jews, and soon after they were boldly upbraiding the Sanhedrin and proclaiming the resurrection of Christ. Consider also their martyrdom. They were crucified (crucified upside down), sawed in half, stoned to death, and killed in many other ways—all except John, who was exiled to the island of Patmos by Nero. Why would they give their lives for what they knew to be false?

Seven, there is the character of Christ Himself. Christ is universally acknowledged, even often enough by skeptics, to be a paragon of virtue—the most noble, moral, truthful, and ethical man the world has ever seen. The last thing Jesus would promote would be deception, including the deception that He rose from the dead—if, in fact, He didn't.

THEORIES THAT TRY TO EXPLAIN AWAY
THE RESURRECTION OF CHRIST

As apologist Josh McDowell points out, some theories to explain away the resurrection of Christ take as much faith to believe as the Resurrection itself.[22] He has debated the Resurrection with skeptics more than just about anybody alive. He writes:

> After more than 700 hours of studying this subject and thoroughly investigating its foundation, I have come to the conclusion that the resurrection of Jesus Christ is one of the most wicked, vicious, heartless hoaxes ever foisted upon the minds of men, or it is the

most fantastic fact of history. . . . A student at the University of Uruguay said to me: "Professor McDowell, why can't you refute Christianity?" I answered, "For a very simple reason: I am not able to explain away an event in history—the resurrection of Jesus Christ."[23]

Let's examine now some of the theories put forth to explain away the resurrection of Jesus Christ.

THE FRAUD THEORY

The first theory—which was and is the theory of the religious leaders in Jerusalem—to explain away Christ's resurrection is called the "Fraud Theory." Essentially, what the Jews are saying is that the whole thing was a fraud. We read: "Now while they were going, behold, some of the guard came into the city and reported to the chief priests all the things that had happened" (Matthew 28:11).

You hear it said sometimes that Jesus never appeared to anybody but believers, but it's not true. He appeared to the guards. They were so terrified by His appearance that they fainted and became as dead men. Then they came and told the high priest what had happened. Jesus appeared to James, his brother, who was skeptical. Jesus appeared to Saul, the persecutor. These people were not Christians at the time.

The Bible continues:

> When they had assembled with the elders and consulted together, they gave a large sum of money to the soldiers, saying, "Tell them 'His disciples came at night and stole Him away while we slept.' And if this comes to the governor's ears, we will appease him and make you secure." So they took the money and did as they were instructed; and this saying is commonly reported among the Jews until this day [. . . even until this day, nearly 2,000 years later] (Matthew 28:12-15).

Let us consider how that stacks up with the evidence. First of all, there is the Christian Church. Does the Fraud Theory give a plausible reason for the Christian Church? The Church was founded by the apostles, who preached the Resurrection. If the Fraud Theory were right, they knew they had stolen the body, but they went ahead and proclaimed that He had risen from the dead.

Something happened to the disciples that changed them in a moment from being cowards to becoming courageous heroes. They said it was that they had seen Jesus risen from the dead. To say that they stole the body and made up a resurrection doesn't make sense. That view does not reflect the realities of human nature. For example, when two criminals are charged with the same murder, even when they have previously been friends, they will almost invariably accuse the other of pulling the trigger. But the disciples didn't change their story one bit, although they had everything to gain and nothing to lose by doing so. The apostles continued throughout all of their lives to proclaim that they had seen Him risen from the dead. Their speaking out led to torture and execution, but none of them ever sought to save his own skin by revealing the "plot."

Dr. Principal Hill, who wrote *Lectures in Divinity*, which was popular in the nineteenth century, has shown the absurdity of the Fraud Theory perhaps more succinctly than anyone else:

> You must suppose that twelve men of mean birth, of no education, living in that humble station which placed ambitious views out of their reach and far from their thoughts, without any aid from the state, formed the noblest scheme which ever entered into the mind of man, adopted the most daring means of executing that scheme, conducted it with such address as to conceal the imposture under the semblance of simplicity and virtue. You must suppose, also, that men guilty of blasphemy and falsehood, united in an attempt the best contrived, and which has in fact proved the most successful for making the world virtuous; that they formed this single enterprise without seeking any advantage to themselves, with an avowed contempt of loss and profit, and with the certain expectation of scorn and persecution; that although conscious of one another's villainy, none of them ever thought of providing for his own security by disclosing the fraud, but that amidst sufferings the most grievous to flesh and blood they persevered in their conspiracy to cheat the world into piety, honesty and benevolence. Truly, they who can swallow such suppositions have no title to object to miracles.[24]

How true that is. No, the Fraud Theory will not stand up to the evidence.

THE SWOON THEORY

A second theory to explain away the Resurrection is the Swoon Theory. This is the theory of the Christian Scientists. The Swoon Theory is the idea that Jesus never really died. It's interesting that until the 1800s, nobody ever thought that Jesus hadn't died.

I think it is significant that the people who put Him to death were "in the business." What was their trade? Their business was taking people who were alive and making them into people who were dead. That is what they did for a living. They would go home at night and say, "Well, I did three today, honey." They were experts at what they did.

But what the Swoon Theory says is that Jesus didn't really die; He merely swooned and then, being placed in the fresh coolness of the tomb, He revived. That does not live up to the facts. Obviously, here is a man who had been scourged, which often killed people in and of itself. His hands and feet and His side had been pierced.

In the Philippines, some people have had themselves crucified on Good Friday. They will sometimes stay up there for three, four, or five minutes, and then—not having been scourged, not having been up all night, not having gone without food for hours, not having had their side and pericardium pierced—they are taken down and to the hospital, where they very nearly die.

Jesus, we are supposed to believe, having been placed in the cool freshness of a tomb, revived. But if a person has gone into shock, should you put him in a cool place? No way. That would kill him. Instead, you cover him with blankets and try to keep his body temperature up. So, the cool freshness of the tomb may sound nice on a hot day, but if you are in shock, that is the last thing a person wants or needs. In fact, if He were not dead when they put Him into the tomb, that most certainly would have killed Him.[25]

Supposedly, He stays there for three days, and then He gets up on mangled feet, hobbles to the door of the tomb and finds this stone weighing a few tons. He places His mangled hands against the flat side of the rock and rolls it away, overcomes the Roman guard of armed men, and takes a seven-mile hike to Emmaus, chatting with the fellows on the way. No one noticed He was limping. Then He treks almost a hundred miles to Galilee, climbs a mountain, and there convinces 500 people that He is the Lord of Life.

The Swoon Theory has received a fatal blow from a skeptic by the name of David Friedrich Strauss—a nineteenth century German who wrote a life of Christ. He didn't believe in the Resurrection, but he knew the Swoon Theory was utterly ridiculous. Listen to what an unbeliever says about this:

> It is impossible that a being who had stolen half dead out of the sepulcher, who crept about, weak and ill, wanting medical treatment, who required bandaging, strengthening, and indulgence, and who, still at last, yielded to his sufferings, could have given to the disciples the impression that he was a conqueror over death and the grave, The Prince of Life, an impression which lay at the bottom of all of their future ministry. Such a resuscitation could only have weakened the impression which he made in life and in death and at the most, could only have given it an elegiac voice, a lament for the dead, but could by no possibility have changed their sorrow into enthusiasm, have elevated their reverence into worship.[26]

With Strauss' critique, the Swoon Theory has swooned away for all but the devoted Christian Scientists.

THE SPIRITUAL RESURRECTION THEORY

Then there is the view of the Jehovah's Witnesses, the Spiritual Resurrection Theory. This theory also seems to be gaining popularity with some theological liberals today. They say that Jesus' resurrection was not physical, but spiritual, and that He was just a spirit. The Bible directly refutes this: "Now as they said these things, Jesus Himself stood in the midst of them, and said to them, 'Peace to you.' But they were terrified and frightened, and supposed they had seen a spirit" (Luke 24:36-37).

Yes, says the Jehovah's Witnesses, they were right. What they saw was a spirit. Not so fast. Luke continues:

> And He said to them, "Why are you troubled? And why do doubts arise in your hearts? Behold My hands and My feet, that it is I Myself. Handle Me and see, for a spirit does not have flesh and bones as you see I have." When He had said this, He showed them His hands and His feet. But while they still did not believe for joy, and marveled, He said to them, "Have you any food here?" So they gave Him a piece of broiled fish and some honeycomb. And He took it and ate in their presence (Luke 24:38-43).

This is not to mention the fact that if Jesus were just a ghost or spirit, then what about the body? Well, the body is still in the tomb. What about the disciples who ran to the tomb when they heard that Jesus had risen? They would have gotten there, and the stone would be in front of the door, and Jesus would still be in the tomb. Well, the Jehovah's Witnesses have managed to take care of that, too, with the same disregard of anything the Scripture or history teaches, and they simply said that God destroyed the body. He evaporated it, so it just disappeared, but there is nothing in the Bible that says anything whatsoever about that.

THE WRONG PERSON THEORY

Fourth, there is the view of the Muslims. This is the Wrong Person Theory. I doubt very much if you ever heard of this because, other than the Muslims, I don't know of anybody that believes it. But the Koran says of Jesus, "They slew him not nor crucified, but it appeared so unto them" (Surah 4:157). They believe that somehow, on Good Friday, there was a mix-up and Judas got crucified. But no eyewitness accounts say that Judas was crucified. Second, we have Mary, His mother, standing at the foot of the Cross for all of those hours looking at Him and weeping over her dying son. He says to her, "Woman, behold thy son!" (John 19:26). According to this theory, she was confused—as were Pilate, the Sanhedrin, and the disciples. Everybody was confused, including Jesus—because He then came to the disciples after He rose from the dead. I wonder who they think appeared to the disciples and said, "Behold my hands and feet?" Do they believe that Judas arose from the dead?

Another fatal flaw to this theory is that it doesn't coincide at all with the character of Jesus. He was a man of impeccable integrity, but according to this theory, He would be a fraud, a deceiver. Furthermore, if this theory were true, the tomb would still be occupied (but we know it's empty); Judas' body would still be in the tomb. What about the guards? What happened to them? When the early Christians declared Jesus risen from the dead, the guards could have easily countered what they said and just showed them the tomb with the Roman seal still affixed. This theory doesn't fit any of the known facts in this case.

THE HALLUCINATION THEORY

Fifth, there is the Hallucination Theory. It holds that all of the disciples simply had hallucinations when they saw Him risen from the dead. Psychologists have pointed out that hallucinations are idiosyncratic[27]—that is, they are very personal and private. People don't have collective hallucinations. Jesus appeared to the people in the morning; He had breakfast with them. They hallucinated having breakfast. He appeared at noon, He walked with them to Emmaus, He appeared with them at suppertime several times, He appeared inside, He appeared outside. He even appeared to 500 people at one time. Not only did they see Him, but also they heard Him, talked to Him, handled Him, and watched Him eat.

Having thus hallucinated that Jesus was alive and had appeared to them, they ran to the tomb and hallucinated that the tomb was empty, the Roman guard was gone, the stone was rolled away, and the grave clothes were empty. Then they began to preach that Jesus rose from the dead. If that were the case, this hallucination would be contagious. They declared that "You, Sanhedrin, you have taken with wicked hands and you have slain the Prince of Life and Glory and God has raised Him from the dead." So, the Sanhedrin ran down to the tomb and had the same hallucination—that it was empty, too.

The Romans, seeing there was a tumult, went down and checked things out and talked to the guard. The guards all had hallucinations that the tomb was empty. This is all ridiculous, obviously. It doesn't deal with any of the evidence.

THE WRONG TOMB THEORY

There is the theory that suggests the women went to the wrong tomb. Again, we must deal with the evidence. It is conceivable that the women got mixed up, and though they had been there on Friday evening, they went to the wrong tomb. According to Kirsopp Lake, a liberal biblical scholar who taught at Harvard (1914-37), this was conceivable in that there were so many tombs around Jerusalem. But I have been to that tomb, and there aren't any tombs around it—nor were there at the time of Christ.

If this theory were correct, the women went to the wrong tomb, Peter and John (by themselves) ran to the wrong tomb, and the disciples went to the wrong tomb. Joseph of Arimathea, who owned the tomb, naturally would want to see what happened, and yet he, too, went to the wrong tomb. The Sanhedrin also was concerned and went to the wrong tomb. Then, the angel came down, and the angel went to the wrong tomb—but what does an angel know about tombs?

Of course, all the while there were the guards saying, "Hey, fellows, we're over here." They, at least, were at the right tomb. Again, this obviously is a wrong theory, and it doesn't answer any of the facts.

If the women and everybody else went to the wrong tomb and started proclaiming Christ risen from the dead, what would the Sanhedrin do? They would go to the right tomb, tell the soldiers to roll back the stone and say, "Bring Him out." Then they would hang His corpse up by the heels in the town square in Jerusalem, and say, "There is your glorious Prince of Life. Take a good whiff of His rotting corpse." That would have been the end of Christianity right then and there.

THE LEGEND THEORY

Lastly, there is the Legend Theory. This is the idea that the "myth" of Christ rising from the dead just sort of gradually grew up over the decades and centuries. This view was popular in the nineteenth century. That was back when they said that the Gospels were written in the second or even the third century by people other than the apostles, but all of that has collapsed in the last 30 or 40 years. Even the late Bishop John A. T. Robinson of England, one of the most blatant critics, wrote a book pointing out that the conservative scholars were right all along, and that the Gospels were written by the men whose names they bear and in the times we have said they were written. Robinson said, near the end of his life, that he believed all the Gospels, including John, were written before 70 A.D.[28]

Furthermore, as stated above, secular historians point out that the Church of Jesus Christ began in 30 A.D. in Jerusalem, because the apostles preached the Resurrection. Jesus and the Resurrection were the central thrust of their teaching, so there was no time for myth-making or legend-spinning. As Peter said, "For we did not follow cunningly devised fables when we made known to you the power and coming of our Lord Jesus Christ, but were eyewitnesses of His majesty" (2 Peter 1:16). John said, speaking of Jesus: "That which was from the beginning, which we have heard, which we have seen with our eyes, which we have looked upon, and our hands have handled, concerning the Word of life ... we declare to you" (1 John 1:1, 3b).

What's more, we know how all of the apostles died. They were crucified and stoned and cut up. All this was done to them supposedly for believing a legend which hadn't even yet developed, which wasn't going to develop for another 100 or 150 years. That's absurd. It doesn't deal with any of the factual information. It doesn't deal with what the Sanhedrin, the Jews and the Romans would have done.

In his book *The Historical Jesus*, Gary Habermas points out that there are 18 different first or second century non-Christian writers who present more than a hundred facts about the birth of Christ, His life, teachings, miracles, crucifixion, resurrection and ascension. They include Josephus, Tacitus, Thallus, Phlegon, Pliny the Younger, Suetonius, Emperor Trajan, Emperor Hadrian, the Talmud, Lucian, Mara Bar-Serapion, and so on.[29] This is no legend that built up over the centuries.

"MIRACLES DON'T HAPPEN"

Some people begin with the assumption that miracles don't happen; therefore, Christ could not have risen from the dead. This doesn't explain any of the facts. This is also circular logic. It's merely a presupposition that disallows the possibility of the Resurrection. Who is open minded here? Surely not people who rejects the Resurrection out of hand because they know miracles don't happen. How can anyone know that miracles don't happen? That's an illogical assumption.

BUT CHRIST HAS RISEN FROM THE DEAD

The truth is that Christ rose from the dead. The greatest problem mankind has ever faced, generation after generation, century after century, millennia after millennia, has been solved by Jesus. Death has been with us since the fall of man, and people have always asked, "If a man dies, will he rise again?" Jesus Christ has given us irrefutable evidence that the answer is "yes." The greatest efforts of the most brilliant, unbelieving skeptical minds of the last 2,000 years to disprove the Resurrection have all come to naught. There is not one of them that could stay afloat in a debate for 15 minutes when the evidence is given a fair examination.

There are other evidences I could discuss at length, if space permitted. I will mention two of them briefly. For example, author Mike Licona has written a book showing that the resurrection of Christ can be proven in history without picking up the New Testament.[30]

Another piece of evidence for the Resurrection is the transformation of the Sabbath from the Jewish Saturday to the Christian Sunday. The Resurrection took place amidst Jews who were committed and zealous Sabbatarians. How is it that suddenly the day of worship changed from the seventh day Sabbath to the first day? Because the resurrection of Jesus Christ from the dead happened on the first day of the week. For these Jews who believed in Jesus (and all the early Christians were Jews) to switch over from strict observance of Saturday as their holy Sabbath to Sunday as the all-important "Lord's day," as it is called in the New Testament, was a monumental shift. The Resurrection was the cause of that shift. Christians have been worshiping Jesus Christ on Sunday from the very beginning to the present.

CONCLUSION

The Apostle Paul had to deal with a first century false teaching going around in the Church at Corinth. Some of the members of that Church were claiming that there was no resurrection of the dead, which would imply that Jesus had not risen from the dead. Paul then wrote the following words, which have assured tens of millions of Christians down through the centuries:

> And if Christ is not risen, then our preaching is empty and your faith is also empty. . . . And if Christ is not risen, your faith is futile; you are still in your sins! Then also those who have fallen asleep in Christ have perished. If in this life only we have hope in Christ, we are of all men the most pitiable. But now Christ is risen from the dead, and has become the firstfruits of those who have fallen asleep (1 Corinthians 15:14, 17-20).

In the early Church, one Christian would greet another with the proclamation, "Jesus is risen." The other would respond, "He is risen indeed," and so we proclaim twenty centuries later: He is risen indeed.

CHAPTER 14

"O DEATH, WHERE IS THY STING?"

For as in Adam all die, even so in Christ all shall be made alive.

1 CORINTHIANS 15:22

PAUL HARVEY, MY FAVORITE NEWS commentator, tells a wonderful story about a pastor in Boston who was walking down the street one day. He saw a little rag-a-muffin boy carrying an old beat-up cage containing several shivering little nondescript birds. The preacher stopped him and said, "Son, where did you get those birds?"

The boy replied, "I trapped them, sir, out in the field."

The preacher asked, "What are you going to do with them?"

The little boy said, "I'm going to play with them."

"Well," said the preacher, "you are going to get tired of playing with them after a while and then what are you going to do with them?"

The boy said, "I've got a cat at home, and the cat likes birds. I think I'll feed them to the cat."

Then the preacher asked the boy, "Son, how much will you take for those birds?"

The boy answered, "Why, Mister, they're no good. They're just old field birds. You wouldn't want them. They can't sing, they aren't pretty, they can't do anything."

The preacher said, "Well, I am willing to buy them. How much would you charge?"

The boy thought for a moment and said, "Two dollars." The

preacher pulled two dollars out of his pocket and gave it to the amazed boy, who disappeared down an alley. The preacher took the birdcage, opened it, and urged the birds one by one out of the cage, and they flew away. The preacher set the cage down beside the pulpit Easter morning and began to tell what seemed to be an unrelated story—a story about the devil in the Garden of Eden and how he trapped two people and then all of their descendants and put them in a cage. He began to play with them, to make them miserable, and Christ said, "What are you going to do with them when you get through playing with them and hurting them?"

The devil replied, "I'm going to kill them. I'm going to damn them."

Christ said, "How much would you take for them?"

The devil said, "All of your sweat and all of your blood," and Jesus paid the price and opened the cage.

Christ delivers us from him who has, through the fear of death, kept the whole world in bondage. Have you felt the bondage of the fear of death, perhaps in the night season, perhaps when you are looking into a grave? It has touched all men in one way or another.

Samuel Johnson was a great intellectual. He gave us the first English dictionary. His house in London was the center of the educated, elite society of that town. All of the authors and poets and other literati gathered together there to share in the scintillating conversation in the home of Samuel Johnson.

One day the discussion turned to the subject of death, and Johnson said he didn't want to discuss that. Some witty sophisticate said, "Well, why not?"

He answered solemnly, "Because, sir, I might be damned."

The man asked, "What in the world could you possibly mean by that?"

Johnson replied, "I mean that I might be condemned by almighty God to eternal and everlasting punishment—that's what I mean. I will hear no more on it," and he rose and left the room—in the bondage of the fear of death. The great Thomas Carlyle said:

Frightful to all men is Death;
from of old named King of Terrors.
Our little compact home of an Existence,
where we dwell complaining,
Yet as in a home, is passing, in dark agonies,
into an Unknown of Separation,
Foreignness, and unconditioned Possibility.

Yes, for those who have thought about it, it is called the King of Terrors. Dryden put it well: "Death, in itself is nothing; but we fear. To be we know not what, we know not where."

Or consider T. S. Eliot, in his masterpiece, *Murder in the Cathedral*, who said: "Not what we call death, but what beyond death is not death, we fear, we fear."

So, if death is the King of Terrors, and life is the greatest possession we have, what can we do about this problem? It is interesting how people have dealt with it. First of all, there are those who have attempted to simply postpone it, to push it back as far as they can. How are we going to do this? By exercise, of course. We need to get in shape, get fit. The best way to do that is to run, and so we had a book on running by "Mr. Running" himself, Jim Fixx, but that idea sort of died down a bit when Jim dropped dead while running.

Aha, it's not what we do; it's what we eat that is important. Vitamins and minerals and herbs by the scores, by the hundreds. That is the secret. At least that is what a book on life extension told us a couple of decades ago. We could live to at least 150 years. Then one of the authors had the temerity to up and die at a reasonably young age, and that theory doesn't have quite the kick it once had.

Then, of course, those in the know realize that the secret is in the water. Why, the discoverer of Florida knew that. Ponce de Leon was looking for the Fountain of Youth, and so have several million "snow birds" in Florida, where I live. I'm afraid that no one has found it.

There are others who simply try to ignore death. They take the ostrich approach that if they just stick their heads in the sand and say it's not there, they won't have to think about it at all. "Ignorance is bliss" is their motto. Again, interestingly, Samuel Johnson said that most men spend all of their time going from one diversion to another, simply trying to avoid thinking about their own mortality. You can't get away for too long with that. Eventually, it catches up.

Third, beyond those who postpone or ignore it, there are those who deny that there is anything to it, that dying is really nothing at all, and that is all there is—nothing at all. The late Corliss Lamont, a leading American humanist, said: "I've come to the conclusion that the life which human beings know on this earth is the only one they will ever know. It seems to me we are justified in regarding immortality as an illusion."

Therefore, you have nothing to fear. There's nothing to it. In fact, it may not be the last enemy to be overcome, but a friend to be welcomed. So, our young people are being taught in school that suicide is a very viable option. It is interesting that we hear some people say that assisted suicide is wrong, and virtually nothing about suicide itself being wrong. If their philosophy is right, and there is nothing after death, what is wrong with suicide? We know that that is not true. The old saying applies here too: It is out of the frying pan . . . and, I'm afraid, into the fire.

Tragically, millions of our young people are being taught this philosophy of life today in our schools. We have suicide training for children— teaching them various ways of doing it. We even have classes where they teach them how to make their own caskets. Of course, they just shrug it off, because it doesn't really mean anything, does it? However, in a recent eight-year period, 39,000 American young people between the ages of 16 and 24 killed themselves (they were well taught in that subject). Tens of thousands more attempted it. No, it is not something that can be ignored, and it cannot be denied. It is very real. After the Columbine tragedy, *ABC-TV News* did a search of their story archives to see if they had covered that school in any previous segment. They had—in 1991—on the subject of Death Education.

I think of an atheist who spent his whole life saying that there was no God, no Heaven, and no Hell. There was nothing. Death was simply the cessation of being. At length, he came to his last day. He was propped up in his bed and his wife was attending him. They were carrying on a conversation, when suddenly he looked beyond her and saw something that was so terrifying to him that his eyes bulged out and his chin fell open. He tried to say something, but could not speak.

His wife screamed and ran out of the room to get help. When she came back, he was still lying there propped against his pillows with his eyes bulging out and his mouth wide open, seeing something so horrific and terrible that he could not even say what it was. However, for him, it was too late. That hollow-eyed, lank-jawed skull with the bony beckoning finger had already come for him.

Thomas Scott was a skeptic and a humanist, like Corliss Lamont, with this exception: He had traveled down the humanist road farther. He had reached the edge of the precipice, and he could feel the ground giving way beneath his feet, and he said this: "Until this moment I thought there was neither God nor a Hell; now I know and feel that there are both and I am doomed to perdition by the just judgment of the Almighty." But it was too late . . . too late.

Those who have been wiser than that know that there is something beyond. Shakespeare, considered one of the most brilliant men who ever lived, put it well in Hamlet's soliloquy, part of which says:

> To die: to sleep—
> To sleep! perchance to dream: ay, there's the rub,
> For in that sleep of death what dreams may come,
> When we have shuffled off this mortal coil,
> Must give us pause. There's the respect
> That makes calamity of so long life.
>
> . . .
>
> But that the dread of something after death,
> The undiscover'd' country, from whose bourn
> No traveller returns; puzzles the will

And makes us rather bear those ills we have
Than fly to others that we know not of?
Thus conscience does make cowards of us all.

Shakespeare himself knew that Jesus Christ is the only true solution to death. Note what the Bard said in his will: "I commend my soul into the hands of God my Creator, hoping and assuredly believing through the only merits of Jesus Christ my Saviour, to be made partaker of life everlasting; and my body to the earth, whereof it is made."[31]

If we cannot deny death—and that is not an option, no matter who you are—then what must we do? We must conquer it. "Conquer death, you say?" Yes. "Well, that is quite a task you are proposing." Yes, it is. I am happy to say I have One who is capable of undertaking and accomplishing that task, and that is Jesus Christ, the great hero of God. He came into this world for the very purpose of destroying him who has the power of death and freeing us from the bondage of the fear of death. He was the One who faced death eye-to-eye and conquered it on the first Easter by rising from the dead. That is why Christ is the greatest person who ever lived, because He conquered the greatest problem mankind has.

Did it ever occur to you that there is no Easter in Islam? There is no Easter in Hinduism. There is no Easter in Buddhism. There is no Easter in Judaism. There is no Easter in Jainism. There is no Easter in the religion of Lao-tse or Zoroastrianism. Only in Christianity. Also, there is no Calvary in any of those. Only Christ, the Son of God, came to die and pay the penalty for all of our sins. And He rose again from the dead to show that God had accepted that payment and that the portals of Paradise had been opened for all who will place their trust in Him and accept Him as their Savior and Lord. They can be free of the fear of death.

I am happy to say to you that by His great victory I have been set free. Shackles have been broken and I, who once was terrified of death, have no fear of it at all, and I have faced it on several occasions.

Are you still in the bondage of fear? You can be set free. Look unto Jesus. Simply trust in Him as your atoning sacrifice, as your Savior from sin, as your only hope of *Heaven*. Abandon all trust in yourself, in your own goodness, your own righteousness—of which you have none—and place your trust in Him. You will come to *know* that you have eternal life and that you will never really die. Jesus Christ, the Conqueror of Death, said, "I am He who lives, and was dead, and behold, I am alive forevermore" (Revelation 1:18). "Because I live, you will live also" [if you trust in me] (John 14:19b).

The secret of life is in the Cross and an open tomb—the only answer to be found in all of the world.

The ancient pagans had no hope. Life was very dreary. They had no expectation that they would rise from the dead. Socrates was, no doubt, one of the most brilliant intellects who ever graced this planet, but at the end of his life, having been condemned by the masters of Athens for perverting the youth, he was given the cup of hemlock to drink. As he breathed his last few breaths, and his eyelids began to flutter, his disciples, who had gathered around, leaned close to ask one last question, "Master, shall we live again?"

"I hope so, but no man can know."

WE NEED NOT FEAR

But we who believe in Jesus know. "These things I have written . . . that you may *know* that you have eternal life" (1 John 5:13; emphasis mine). Jesus said, "Because I live, you will live also" (John 14:19). Jesus Christ's resurrection is the first fruits of them that slept. That is something all Christians can know. He can know that because Christ suffered and died for our sins and rose again from the dead that we can live with Him forever. Not only that, we need not fear the grave.

When Jesus was born, the angels said, "Fear not." When the angel appeared at the tomb, he said to the women, "Fear not." When Jesus appeared to John, he said, "Fear not." Jesus can take away the fear. He breaks the bands of death, and destroys the power of Satan, who has kept humankind in bondage through fear of death. I have faced death, and I have been 100 percent unafraid—not because I am a hero, but because I trust in the greatest Hero who ever was.

I remember one time being on an airplane where we experienced terrible turbulence. It was the kind of ride where you literally expected that any minute could be your last. By the grace of God, I was very calm, and a passenger asked me how in the world I could remain so calm in the face of death. I replied, "Oh, that's simple. If this plane goes down, I go up." I was able to share the Gospel with my fellow traveler.

Jesus confronted death in its own domain and destroyed the power of Satan. The angels came down and not only rolled away the stone, but sat upon it, as if they were saying, "Death, O Death, O Hell, O Hades, O devil, who will roll this stone back again? Come and try it if you can." Death, the King of Terrors, has been destroyed.

> Who shall rebuild for the tyrant his prison?
> The scepter lies broken that fell from his hands.
> His dominion is ended; our Lord is arisen
> The helpless shall soon be released from their bands.

Death has lost its sting.

A father and two boys were out for a picnic in a woods one day. A huge bumblebee came buzzing around and stung one of the boys on the arm. He cried out in pain as he rolled around on the ground. Then the bee began to buzz around the other boy and he was flailing and screaming and crying and running. The father said to him, "Son, don't run, don't cry, don't be afraid. The bee has left his stinger in your brother."

So death has left its sting in our elder brother, Jesus Christ, our Savior from sin. All of that power of death was unleashed upon Him so that we may not have fear.

The Apostle Paul reviewed the significance of the resurrection of Jesus Christ in the magnificent chapter on the issue, 1 Corinthians 15. In that passage he asks the question, "O death, where is thy sting? O grave, where is thy victory?" (v. 55 KJV). The sting is lost. The victory belongs to the Son of God who has triumphed in His passion and resurrection.

As we consider the power of the passion and its triumphant results, we have one last look at the resurrection of Christ over the grave. There is a remarkable artifact from antiquity that many who have studied it believe provides *scientific* evidence for the Resurrection.

CHAPTER 15

IS THERE SCIENTIFIC EVIDENCE FOR THE RESURRECTION OF CHRIST?

And she brought forth her firstborn Son, and wrapped
Him in swaddling cloths, and laid Him in a manger,
because there was no room for them in the inn.

LUKE 2:7

ON CHRISTMAS MORNING, IN MILLIONS of homes around the country, bows and wrappings of all sorts will be flying around in profusion, as eager young people commit mayhem on carefully wrapped and beribboned packages. Now and again there will be found under the tree a package that has been wrapped beautifully and so delightfully that someone might say, "Wait, save that wrapping. Save it for possible future use." I am sure we have all seen that happen at one time or another. The wrappings on some packages are just too pretty to throw away.

Another thing that happens at Christmastime is that some people do not like what they have received, so after Christmas they line up to take the gifts back, just as they lined up to buy them in the first place. Of course, by then, the ribbons and wrappings have all been torn up. They are not wrapped neatly, but are usually shoved in some old brown paper bag and taken back to the store.

Ribbons and wrapping are so much a part of our Christmas tradition. As I thought about this, it occurred to me that maybe there is a "word" in the wrappings. Could there be? If so, what might that be?

As I searched the Scriptures, I noted that God's great Christmas gift to humankind, His own Son, was wrapped. We are told: "And she brought forth her firstborn Son and wrapped Him in swaddling cloths." So, before being presented to the world, God's Christmas gift also was wrapped. In thinking further on this, it came to me that the world did not like the Christmas gift from God and sent it back.

Most people, however, have the courtesy and good taste not to have damaged the presents when they take them back to the store. God's Christmas gift, however, was used, bruised, and abused before it was sent back. Interestingly, we find that it, too, was wrapped before it was returned. We read that Joseph of Arimathea wrapped Him in a clean linen cloth.

Fascinatingly, the claim has been made for some time that the wrapping in which the gift of God was sent back to Heaven has been saved. I speak of what is known as the Shroud of Turin, which many claim is the actual burial shroud provided by Joseph of Arimathea, in which the body of Jesus was wrapped before burial. That wrapping has been subjected to the most intensive scientific scrutiny ever placed upon any artifact in history.

Is this wrapping actually the burial shroud of Christ, or is it some sort of pious hoax perpetrated by a medieval artist? It is worth our examining today. Is this shroud real? Is this further evidence that has been attested to by science confirming the message of the Bible given us? Or is this a fraud?

I should confess that when I first heard about the so-called Shroud of Turin, my attitude was one of great skepticism. I have never been impressed with relics. There are enough pieces around of the "genuine" Cross of Christ to build Noah's ark, and there are at least forty other shrouds that are claimed to be the shroud of Christ. Was this any different? I, for one, did not think so at all. However, it should be required of every honest person—certainly of every Christian—to have an open mind and to examine the evidence. Christianity is based upon evidence. What does the evidence say? It was with interest that I heard about the earlier photographic examinations that had been made by some Italian scientists.

In 1978 the Shroud of Turin Research Project (STURP) was formed. The group was composed of thirty-three scientists, most of them American, who came from the space research laboratories, from computer analysis team, and from every type of microscopic, spectroscopic, photographic, and analytical discipline. They sought permission to scientifically scrutinize the Shroud as no religious artifact had ever been examined before.

Before I tell you what the results were, let me give you the history of the Shroud and the person whose image is indelibly affixed to it. The Shroud of Turin can be positively traced back to 1357 A.D., when it was displayed for the first time in Lirey, France, by the house of Geoffrey de Charny. When it was displayed, the bishop of the area was incensed at the idea of some middle-class family in his area actually possessing the genuine shroud of Christ. He stopped the exhibition and refused to have it shown any further.

In 1449 the granddaughter of the deceased de Charny displayed it again. The succeeding bishop again tried to have the exhibition stopped. It was termed a fraud. It was said to have been painted by a cunning artist.

There are some "sindonologists" (those who study the Shroud) who believe it can be traced back to about 1000 A.D. in Constantinople and to Edessa, where it may be traced all the way back to the first century. Further, a pollenologist (one who studies the various spores or pollens produced by seed-bearing plants) examined the pollens that were taken off the Shroud, and found about forty-five or forty-six of them from France, more from Turkey, and the vast majority from Palestine. Furthermore, the Shroud itself was made of linen, but it was microscopically detected that there were pieces of cotton also within, indicating it had been woven on a loom that had also been used to weave cotton. Cotton was not produced in Europe in the Middle Ages, though it was plentiful in the Middle East. Indeed the plot began to thicken.

WHAT IS THE SHROUD OF TURIN?

The Shroud measures three and one half feet wide and fourteen feet long. It was apparently placed under and over the entire body of the man represented in the Shroud, covering him down to his feet. On the Shroud is a minutely detailed and accurate picture of the entire body of this person—both the front and back. I am sure most of you have seen a picture of that face and that body. The man is lying with his hands folded across the pelvic area.

The image of a man is identified by ethnologists as a Semite, having the features of a Jew. He is approximately 5'10" tall and about 175 pounds in weight. He is a man who has suffered a very violent death. He is unclothed. He has been horribly flogged. Unquestionably, the man was flogged with the Roman *flagrum* (or *flagellum*), which was a whip made out of three long pieces of rawhide with a wooden handle. At the end of each piece of rawhide is a tiny piece of lead shaped like a bow tie and held in the middle with the thong (sometimes sharp pieces of bone were used). There are at least a hundred and twenty or more indentations indicated on the Shroud, where virtually every part of the body is covered with these. In this particular case, these pieces of lead were actually sharpened so that they bit more deeply into the flesh.

What we see is a picture of a person who has been terribly flogged and scourged. It is ascertained by the medical examiners of the Shroud that this Man was flogged by two individuals who stood on either side of Him and alternated blows, one of whom was taller than the other and one of whom scourged Him more fiercely and savagely than did the other. The scourging went all the way down to the ankles and up to the neck.

Furthermore, we see that this is a Man who has been crowned with thorns—not the usual ringlet depicted in Christian art—that were pressed down on His head, producing innumerable puncture wounds all over the forehead and head, which bled profusely over the face. We note also that part of the beard had been plucked out.

An artist's rendering of the picture on the Shroud produces precisely that traditional picture you see of Jesus. Either a cunning craftsman in the fourteenth century put the traditional picture of Jesus on the Shroud or else the Shroud has been the source of the traditional pictures of Jesus that we have known through the centuries. It is one or the other. We will note later (in discussing a sixth century icon) that clearly, the Shroud came first and then our image of what we think Jesus looked like.

We see that this person had been beaten in the face before He was crucified. His left eye is almost swollen shut. He has contusions on his chin and several places on His face. Furthermore, we see that across His shoulders, a heavy weight of some sort had been placed because there are abrasions that scrape away the marks left by the scourging. Apparently, He had had a violent fall. There are cuts on both knees and a deep cut on the left knee. Furthermore, the left septum had been violently torn from the face. His nose had been broken, as if He had fallen with no effort to break the fall with His hands.

THE HORRORS OF CRUCIFIXION

We also note that the man has been crucified in the feet and hands. The left foot is placed over the right and a single spike has pierced them both. In the case of His hands, the spikes are found at the base of the hand, the beginning of the wrist, between the radius and ulna. It is interesting that traditional Christian art has always shown Christ with the spikes in the palms.

Inspired by the Shroud and the fact that the wrists, not the palms, were pierced, a French physician decided to see which was correct—traditional Christian art or the Shroud of Turin. Dr. Pierre Barbet, in the early part of the twentieth century, experimented with corpses, actually crucifying them, and found that nails in the palms ripped out easily and were incapable of supporting the weight of a human being.[32]

Further excavations have revealed that other victims of Roman crucifixion were indeed pierced at the base of the hands or the wrist. Furthermore, the Greek word *cheir* and the Hebrew word *yad* both mean "hand," "wrist," or "forearm." Therefore, the Shroud is not contrary to the teaching of the Scriptures, but contrary to the generally accepted view that has been held until recent excavations. So the Shroud is historically correct—not traditional Christian art—in that the nails went through the wrists.

We further note that the man has been pierced in the right side with a wound that is one and three-fourths inches long and seven-sixteenths of an inch wide, which happens to fit exactly with an extant Roman *lancea*—the lance with a leaf-shaped blade that was used by Roman centurions. This is, indeed, an amazing coincidence.

We might also note that the legs of this man in the Shroud were not broken, as was the custom. Once his legs were broken, the crucified person could no longer lift himself up, causing the pectoral muscles to become paralyzed. When that happened, he was unable to exhale and was soon asphyxiated. The person was constantly raising himself up on the spike by straightening his knees and then collapsing in agony and continued to do this all the hours he was on the Cross. In the case of the man in the Shroud, there are two streams of blood on the arm, ten degrees apart, showing that He was in both the elevated and the collapsed positions. However, his legs were not broken.

These are amazing descriptions, completely in harmony in every single detail of what we know historically and biblically of the death and crucifixion of Christ.

We might also note this: Jesus received a burial according to the Jewish custom, but only in part. He was covered with a shroud, as the Bible says. It also indicated that there was a napkin or cloth placed around his head. Generally, it has been thought that this napkin covered his face. Scientists now believe this was a napkin wrapped into a roll and tied around the head in order to close the mouth. Jewish ritual commands that this be done, so rigor mortis would not set in with the person's mouth agape. In fact, there is a separation on the left side of the beard, indicating that something is covering part of the beard, which is believed to be the headband to keep the mouth closed. There is a cloth in Spain, the Sudarium of Oviedo, which is believed to be the head cloth used to wrap the face of Christ. Furthermore, scientists have found that the bloodstains on the Sudarium can be matched up with the bloodstains on the Shroud.

It has now been discovered that coins covered the eyes, as was the Jewish custom of that time. These coins had been discovered by the late Father Francis Filas to be "leptons" that were minted in Judea between 29 and 31 A.D. by Pontius Pilate. Christ was crucified in the year 30 A.D.[33]—a remarkable coincidence, indeed.

We can see that the burial was incomplete and that the body was not washed. We know the Sabbath was coming on, and they had to stop their burial proceedings. The women returned early Sunday morning to complete them, but Jesus had risen from the dead. We find that in all these details the Shroud matches what we know from the Scriptures.

The question now is: Is it a cunningly devised portrait painted by some clever medieval artist? Wasn't it widely reported in 1988, when they carbon-dated the Shroud that whatever its origin, it dated only from about 1300 A.D?

CARBON DATING AND THE SHROUD

While the carbon dating test in 1988 seemed to indicate the Shroud was of medieval origin, there are many who dispute that test on several reasonable grounds; most notably, they object to where—on the Shroud itself—they selected the samples to test. The 1978 STURP (The Shroud of Turin Research Project) group called for a protocol involving seven samples chosen from various spots around the Shroud. That protocol was violated. Instead, three samples were all taken from the same spot. Which spot? Perhaps a rewoven part of the cloth. During the Middle Ages, the Shroud was often put on public display. Nuns had sewn parts of the cloth in a way that the Shroud could be held up on its side by several poles. The opinion here is that the portion of the Shroud used in the dating isn't authentically from the Shroud itself, but from one of the rewoven parts of the cloth. Note that there are thousands of scientific tests that argue for the Shroud's authenticity. To my knowledge, one test alone—the carbon dating test—argues that it's a fraud.

Archaeologist William Meacham warned before the carbon-14 dating of 1988 to not take such a test too seriously:

> There seems to be an unhealthy consensus approaching the level of dogma among both scientists and lay commentators that C-14 dating will settle the issue once and for all time. This attitude simply contradicts the general perspective of field archaeologists and geologists who view contamination as a very serious problem.[34]

Sindonologist Joseph Marino says:

> ... the sample containing the frontal image; this corner is the most contaminated area of the Shroud. This is the area that has been constantly handled whenever the Shroud has been taken out for exhibits and private showings."[35]

Dr. Alan Whanger, retired Duke Medical School professor and respected sindonologist since the late 1970s, and his wife Mary, wrote this about the carbon dating:

> Contrary to much public opinion, carbon 14 dating is not an exact science. . . . A major reason why obtaining an accurate carbon dating for the Shroud is so difficult is that it has been in the open, moved from place to place, and handled by hundreds of people. Most artifacts, to be dated, have been buried in one spot for thousands of years and are then taken directly to the laboratory. But the Shroud has been in contact with oils, wax, soaps, paints, ointments, open wounds, saliva, sweat, pollens, flowers and other plant parts, organic carbon compounds, microscopic fungi and bacteria, and insect debris.[36]

Carbon-14 dating in general is not always as accurate as many people believe. In his book *The Resurrection of the Shroud*, author Marc Antonacci highlights just a few of the many errors of carbon-14 dating:

- dating of living snail shells to be twenty-six thousand years old
- dating a newly killed seal to be thirteen hundred years old
- dating one-year-old leaves as four hundred years old
- dating a Viking horn to the future year of 2006[37]

Here we see carbon-14 dating is not always so accurate. Even *TIME* magazine reported in a cover story on the Shroud, ten years after the 1988 carbon dating: "It is obviously within the realm of possibility that the radiocarbon tests on the Shroud of Turin were faulty. . . . questions regarding the typicality of the sample swatch cannot be summarily dismissed."[38]

In short, the carbon dating testing, which seemed to discredit the Shroud in 1988 as a medieval forgery, was blown out of proportion. The media strikes again.

INTENSE STUDY OF THE SHROUD

Thirty-three scientists went to Italy in 1978. They brought with them 72 crates of millions of dollars worth of the most sophisticated scientific instruments, and for five days, twenty-four hours a day, in shifts, they exposed that Shroud to every conceivable scientific test. They spent three years analyzing their findings. Though many articles have come out at different times, one thing is definite: In reading the findings of this scientific team, it becomes very clear that all the previous reports are either incomplete, completely inaccurate, or contain false information.

For example, their most conclusive finding of all is that there is no pigment, no dye, no ink, no foreign substance of any kind whatsoever that could produce this incredibly detailed figure of the dorsal and frontal aspect of this entire human being. Their most overwhelming conclusive determination is that it was not produced by the application of anything of any sort to the Shroud. There is nothing there, which is an astonishing revelation. Under the most exhaustive microscopic X-ray and every kind of test, they found nothing there that produces that image.

In fact, what produces the image is what is not there. What is not there is the fact that some of the fibrils of the individual linen threads are dehydrated. It is this dehydrating that produces the yellow tint that produces the picture of the Shroud. Intensities of color are not there. They are all exactly the same. The only difference in tint is due to the fact that in some places there are more dehydrated threads than others. Furthermore, this dehydration is superficial. Each tiny thread is made up of two hundred fibrils, and the superficial nature of the imprint is such that it goes only two or three fibrils deep. It has been totally beyond any modern scientific technique known to be able to produce an image on the Shroud which is that superficial. If you turn the Shroud over, there is no image at all.

Thirdly, they discovered when they used the VP-8 Image Analyzer (an analyzer which is used by NASA to examine light from stars and pictures of planets, turning it into three dimensional images), they found that the image on this Shroud turns into a three-dimensional picture of a human being. It is very impressive to see the three-dimensional figure leap out at you. It is interesting that none of the pictures and photographs and paintings of Jesus, when the same analyzer is used, produce a three-dimensional portrait. A portrait of any kind comes off distorted when put through this analyzer—not so with the Shroud of Turin.

In 1898, when the very first picture of it was taken, photographer Secundo Pia discovered in the dark room, as he developed the glass plate of the negative, that he held in his hands a photographic positive. He discovered that the Shroud essentially contains the properties of a photographic negative. Bear in mind that in 1357, photography had never even been dreamed of, and the concept of negativity and positivity was not even known. Yet, the Shroud of Turin is a photographic negative, so when the first photograph was taken, suddenly, for the first time, the figure leaped out in all its graphic details. It had never been seen that way before.

We find, also, that the image is completely directionless. There is no indication of brushwork upon it. The image is just there. Furthermore, there is no capillary flow. There is no indication of anything ever having been put on it that could have flowed into any of the fibrils or any of the threads, as any substance would tend to do. It is thermally stable, chemically stable, water stable. Researchers have thus concluded that the image was not produced by paint of any sort, by dyes, powders, spices, or any other substances on the Shroud itself.

Furthermore, earlier reports had indicated that what appears to be blood on the Shroud was not actually blood. One of the conclusions of the latest careful and complete examinations is that *it is undoubtedly human blood.*

INTERESTING CONCLUSIONS

We find that very interesting conclusions can be drawn from these studies. Here was a man who was a Jew, who was first flogged, who was crowned with thorns, and who was crucified by the Romans. We know of no one in history, other than Jesus, being crucified after first being crowned with thorns and then later being pierced in the side. We know of no other person whose legs were not broken and whose beard was plucked. When all these factors were computed by probability scientists, the conclusion was that the probabilities were 1 in 225 billion that this was some person other than Jesus of Nazareth. Scientists will never say that this was Jesus. They operate on probabilities, and those are extraordinarily high probabilities. Chemist Alan Adler, who was one of the members of the STURP team that investigated the Shroud so thoroughly in 1978, put it well when he said in *TIME* magazine: "Science can never authenticate this cloth, because there's no lab test for Christ-ness."[39]

There are other conclusions that can be reached. In the nineteenth century, there was devised a Swoon Theory (already discussed in a previous chapter) which said that Jesus never died; therefore, He did not rise from the dead, but was simply revived. One thing the scientists have absolutely concluded is that whoever that man in the Shroud was, he was dead. Rigor mortis had already set in. His left knee is bent slightly, where one foot had been placed on top of the other. His head, through rigor mortis, is bent slightly forward. We read in the Scripture that Jesus, having bowed His head, gave up the ghost. We see that medical examiners and coroners, having examined on the Shroud the spear wound in His side, have conclusively determined that the spear passed through the pericardium and also through the heart. There is no doubt about the fact that when that spear did indeed pierce His side, the blood did not pump out, as it would have from a living heart. The blood oozed out as from a heart that had stopped.

Furthermore, we see that blood had obviously collected and had begun to separate into its constituent parts of red blood corpuscles and white watery serum, because the stains of blood that flowed from the wound had gathered in the middle and spread across the back. Around the edge of them is the clear indication that the blood had divided into its elements. Therefore, there is not a doubt that the man in the Shroud was unquestionably dead.

There is also evidence here for the Resurrection. First of all, there is the cause of the image. What created it? Since the team had decided not to look for a supernatural origin to anything, some of the scientists on the team concluded that there is no known possible natural cause for the image on that shroud. That does leave a supernatural cause. There are those who have speculated that at the moment of His resurrection, Jesus emitted a burst of energy of such a nature that could have produced the scorch on the Shroud, leaving this detailed image.

Furthermore, we see that there was no decomposition in the body. This lines up with the Bible. We also see that the bloodstains, whether they were clots of blood or the thin rivulets of blood that had come down from the wrists and the feet, would undoubtedly be broken or smeared if a shroud were taken off of a body where the blood had dried. This has been proved by repeated tests. We notice that in each of the little rivulets of blood and each of the blood clots, there is not the slightest hint, when examined microscopically, of even the edges of these bloodstains being cracked or broken in the slightest way, which is to say that the scientists have no conception of how that shroud was taken off the body. It could not happen, and yet it did. In short, he appears to have gone right through the cloth.

Lastly, we see that there is a complete correspondence and confirmation of all the biblical details of His suffering, His crucifixion, His burial, and His resurrection. It seems that God has given us another amazing confirmation of His Word. In this day of rampant skepticism, atheism, and unbelief, God seems to be delighting in raising up first one thing and then another to confound the skeptic and the unbeliever to show that His Word is true.

Thank God that He, in His amazing providence, seems to have said, "Save that wrapping for possible future use."

A PLAUSIBLE HISTORY OF THE SHROUD OF TURIN

The Shroud of Turin showed up in 1357 in Lirey, France, in the possession of a family of crusaders. Prior to that, it had been stolen by French crusaders in the early thirteenth century, when they sacked Constantinople. Historian Ian Wilson has made a strong case that the Shroud left Jerusalem in 30 A.D. and traveled up to Edessa in modern-day Turkey. Initially, the Shroud was welcomed by the king (Abgar V), whose contact with it reportedly cured his leprosy. When a later king took over some 20 years later, about 57 A.D., he rejected the Christian faith and persecuted the followers of it. Some of them hid the cloth in the city walls, where it was not discovered until 525 A.D., when workmen were repairing the walls after damage from a flood. They hid it so well that it was hermetically sealed. During this 500-year absence of the Shroud, pictures and images of Jesus Christ were in no way uniform. Christ often appeared beardless and not in any way like we think of Him today. However, from 525 to the present, virtually every image of Jesus is the same. Why? Because they are patterned after the Shroud.

The shroud discovered in 525 was known for its first 1,200 years as the Mandylion. It contained an image "not made by human hands." The cloth was folded in such a way that only the face was showing. That helps to explain why details, such as the nail prints at the wrists and not in the palms, were not known for centuries while, indeed, the likeness of the face was duplicated repeatedly. Those who believe the Shroud is the authentic burial cloth of Jesus Christ also believe that the Mandylion and the Shroud of Turin are one and the same.

Continuing with the Shroud's history, the story is nearly complete. In the tenth century, a Byzantine Army surrounded the small city of Edessa and demanded the holy relic. After a long siege, the Byzantine forces seized their prized quarry and, amid great fanfare, brought the cloth to Constantinople, the capital city. Note that within a hundred years of this event, the Muslims completely destroyed the Christian city of Edessa and changed the name of the town to Urfa. They destroyed some 350 churches of Edessa, including the one that housed the cloth known as the Mandylion. It is likely that the Mandylion/Turin Shroud would have been destroyed, had the Byzantines not seized it.

Then in the early 1200s again, crusading Frenchmen robbed the Byzantines of the treasure. During one of the crusades, the "soldiers of the Cross" (many coming from France) turned on their fellow Christians and sacked Constantinople. In the melee that followed, the prized cloth was missing. Note that within 250 years, the Muslims destroyed the Christian civilization of Constantinople in 1453 and changed the name to Istanbul. They not only killed thousands upon thousands of Christians, they also destroyed many of their works of art, considered by the conquerors to be idolatrous.

Again, it is highly possible the Shroud would have been destroyed, had it not been seized by the French crusaders. More than a hundred years passed, and the cloth showed up in the sleepy village of Lirey, France, in a crusader's family. We know where it has been ever since 1357. It has been under close supervision since then. It was moved to its present location, Turin, Italy, in the late 1500s. Contrary to some popular misconceptions, the Shroud has only belonged to the Roman Catholic Church since 1983.[40]

SOME SPECIFIC DETAILS ABOUT THE SHROUD

Here are some facts about the Shroud worth bearing in mind. Much of this recaps what we discussed above:

- The human anatomy represented on the Shroud is 100 percent correct. Knowledge about anatomy on the Shroud includes details that weren't known until the twentieth century. In contrast, fourteenth century knowledge of anatomy was quite limited. If the cloth were the work of a medieval forger, he knew things that weren't known until centuries later.

- The Shroud was photographed for the first time in 1898, and it was discovered to be a photographic negative. Thus, hundreds of years before photography was invented, here was a photographic negative.

- The photographing of the Shroud led to all sorts of scientific experiments. The vast majority of them—virtually all, in fact—argue for its authenticity, except for one highly publicized experiment (the carbon-14 dating of 1988, which critics argue drew from only one sample and, at that, a rewoven part of the Shroud). The carbon-14 testing concluded that the Shroud must have been a hoax, because it was dated to about 1300 or so. Of the thousands of scientific studies on the Shroud, virtually all of which have argued for its authenticity, guess which one the media picked up on?

- The faint image on the Shroud was not painted on. It was lightly burned on. It is as if at the moment of the Resurrection, Christ's body let off a burst of radiation, as it changed from mortal to immortal. The image on the Shroud is created by some sort of scorching process, yet it is only lightly scorched (in a way that didn't destroy the cloth). The image is only .005 of an inch thick. Although there are a few traces of pigment on the Shroud (because as a holy relic, they put paintings in contact with it, presumably to receive a blessing or the like), the image is not composed of pigment or paint.

- The blood on the Shroud is real human blood. The man in the cloth did not see decay. He was sandwiched inside that cloth for less than 72 hours, yet the blood was undisturbed, which means he somehow went through the cloth; it was not yanked off.

- What you and I think Jesus looked like is based on the Shroud of Turin. People have a universal picture of how they think Jesus looked. Most people don't realize, though, that that image is based on the Shroud of Turin. In fact, when the Shroud was hidden away for several centuries—lest it be destroyed by the pagan rulers—pictures of Jesus, as found in the catacombs, varied. (We would not recognize Him as Jesus.) After the Shroud was unearthed in 525 A.D., virtually all pictures of Jesus—icons, coins, etc.,—began to be patterned after the Shroud. From the sixth century to the present, what we think Jesus looked like is based on the Shroud.

- Dr. Alan Whanger, retired professor at Duke Medical Center, has studied this issue in great depth. He said that while it takes 14 "points of congruence" to prove the identity of fingerprints in a court of law, the Shroud and a sixth century icon (Christ Pantocrator, 550 A.D.) contain more than 250 points of congruence.

- The Shroud has caused some liberals and unbelievers to convert to Christianity. Today, there are many "Bible scholars" who deny the Resurrection. One modern scholar was John A. T. Robinson, a leading clergyman from England, who made quite a splash when he wrote the anti-faith book *Honest To God*. (Robert Funk, founder and director of the Jesus Seminar, indirectly honored him by naming his book after the same pattern; Funk's book is called *Honest to Jesus.*) In 1964, when Robinson's book came out, he was a leading clergyman of the Church of England, essentially telling the whole world he didn't believe, and that it was irrational to believe in Jesus. However, in the last decade of his life, he had a conversion. He became born again. What changed him? The scientific evidence for the Resurrection as based on the Shroud.

- There is a lot of nonsense surrounding the Shroud—people worshiping it as they worship images and light candles—but to dismiss the Shroud because of that is simply guilt by association. The twentieth and twenty-first century scientific studies on the Shroud stand on their own. The Shroud has been studied more rigorously and put through more scientific tests than any artifact in history. Similarly, some Protestants, disagreeing with Catholics on many issues, dismiss the Shroud because it is supposedly Catholic. This, too, is the logical fallacy of guilt by association. Again, the facts on the Shroud stand on their own.

- While leading evangelicals are often silent about the Shroud, and I respect that, *I still think people should look into it for themselves*, because the evidence is there, on yet another front, declaring the Easter message that Jesus is risen.

- In the Middle Ages (and even sometimes today), artistic representations of the crucifixion place the nails in the palms. Yet, the Shroud of Turin places the nails in the wrists. It has now been medically proven that nails in the palms would not suffice to hold a crucified man. It was the Shroud that initiated the medical inquiry into this subject in the first place. The remains of a crucified man found in Israel in 1967 show the nails in the wrists as well.

- The image of the Shroud is three-dimensional. When ordinary photos or paintings are studied through a specific NASA space-age machine (a "VP-8 Image Analyzer"), the image always becomes distorted. However, the Shroud has been proven to have three-dimensional properties. It could not have been a painting.

- The theories of skeptics put forward to explain away the Shroud pay indirect homage to its awesome properties. For example, one recent book proposed that no less a genius than Leonardo da Vinci produced the Shroud—and that he had to secretly crucify a man in the process. However, da Vinci lived about a hundred years after the Shroud appeared. Leonardo was born in 1452, and, again, we know where the Shroud has been since 1357. So there goes another theory. Everyone who studies the Shroud of Turin agrees that this is a mystery not easily explained away. I find it fascinating that some modern scientists with sophisticated laboratory equipment set out to show how some ingenious medieval forger could have created what would be the greatest forgery of all time (if it weren't genuine), using all sorts of elaborate machines and testing data that such an artist didn't have available to him. Then they declare to the world that they have supposedly solved the mystery of the Shroud.

- If it's a hoax, this is no ordinary hoax. The greater evidence argues for its authenticity. As some scientists put it, the Shroud is, if you will, a "snapshot of the Resurrection." At the very moment Christ rose from the dead, something happened—a burst of radiation perhaps—that left a permanent mark on the front and back of the burial cloth that sandwiched the man of the Shroud, who wouldn't stay buried for long. In short, the best theory is that the Shroud of Turin provides scientific evidence for the resurrection of Christ.

FURTHER READING

Please note that I believe in the resurrection of Jesus Christ, apart from what I learn from the Shroud of Turin. If somehow the Shroud were proven beyond all reasonable doubt to be phony, my belief in the Resurrection would continue to stand. The scientific data I learn about that artifact only adds to my belief in Christ's passing from death to life.

Meanwhile, the more I read about the Shroud—even the cockamamie theories put forth to explain it away—the more I believe it is genuine, that it sandwiched Jesus after His death, that He went through it, and that it survived all these centuries to our scientific age in order to provide space-age evidence that Jesus Christ rose from the dead.

New books are coming out all the time about the Shroud—this includes many positive books that confirm that it was, indeed, the burial cloth of Christ. Let me steer the interested reader toward a few of these. I highly recommend the work of Alan and Mary Whanger. Dr. Alan Whanger has applied both his knowledge of the human body and his passion for photography to his studies on the Shroud. Together, he and his wife Mary have written *The Shroud of Turin: An Adventure of Discovery* (Franklin, Tennessee: Providence House, 1998).

In addition, I recommend a book by an attorney, Marc Antonacci, *The Resurrection of the Shroud: New Scientific, Medical and Archaeological Evidence* (New York: M. Evans and Company, Inc., 2000). This book conveys the author's grasp of all the complicated scientific disciplines involved. Antonacci says that if a medieval artist put the Shroud together, look what he would have had to accomplish: "Such an artist would have had to have a knowledge of light negativity, light spectrometry, microscopy, radiology, human physiology, pathology, hematology, endocrinology, forensics, and archaeology. In fact, even with all the technology available to us today at the dawn of the twenty-first century, the Shroud's unique characteristics still cannot be duplicated."[41]

Also, the work of sindonologist Ian Wilson on the Shroud has been groundbreaking. His latest book is recommended—*The Blood and the Shroud: New Evidence That the World's Most Sacred Relic Is Real* (New York: Free Press, 1998). Wilson says about the Turin Shroud: "To try to interpret it as the product of some unknown medieval faker seems rather like arguing for the Taj Mahal being a mere geological accident."[42]

Anyone who takes the time to study the details about the Shroud realizes that it is no ordinary artifact. The more we study it, the more confirmed I think is the conclusion: it is the genuine burial cloth of Jesus Christ, and it provides scientific evidence for His resurrection.

CHAPTER 16

FOOTPRINTS IN THE SANDS OF TIME

Therefore, if anyone is in Christ, he is a new creation;
old things have passed away; behold, all things
have become new

2 CORINTHIANS 5:17

YOU ARE STANDING ON THE beach of a tropical island. As far as you can see down this untouched beach, there is not a single person, so you start walking. It is a beautiful day. The sun is shining brightly, the air is cool, and you walk for mile after mile. Finally, you come to an out-cropping of rock that goes right down into the water and stops your advance. You climb up on the rocks, walk out on the rock pier, and sit down to enjoy the sun. You look down into the clear water and occa-sionally see a beautiful tropical fish swim by.

After a brief rest, you get up, walk back to the beach, jump down on the sand, and start your return. Then you notice, to your amaze-ment, that all of your footprints have disappeared. You had not noticed that the tide has been coming in and has washed them all away, leav-ing not a trace of the fact you ever traversed that beach at all. I thought that to be a pretty good picture of the lives many people live. When it is all over, it is washed away and disappears entirely, leaving not a trace.

However, the passion of Christ gives life purpose, a reason for being. It empowers us with the true meaning for which we were cre-ated and placed on earth: "to glorify God and enjoy Him forever."[43]

We are here to know Christ and to make Him known. What a fulfilling and significant life is ours when we plug into God's plan. Again, all of this, just like our salvation, is made possible only because of Christ's passion. Through Him, we can leave permanent reminders of our having passed through here on earth—especially as we invest in the lives of other people, directly or indirectly steering them toward Jesus Christ.

THE NEED FOR SIGNIFICANCE

I recall reading about a radical South American college student who was asked why he was engaged in these radical activities. He said it was because he was terribly afraid he would die before anybody knew he was alive.

The subject is *significance*. There is something deep down in the crypt of every human soul, a desire planted there by God, for some kind of significance, meaning, and importance to one's life—that life should count for something, that you should make a difference because you were here, that things should be better, that you would leave your footprints—not in sand, but in stone.

How can we find that significance to our lives? There have been a number of ways people have tried. Some have built great memorials for themselves to perpetuate their memories. For example, many of us may have seen the great pyramid at Giza, the greatest of all the pyramids in Egypt. It is an enormous structure. Herodotus, the Greek historian, says it took 400,000 men working day and night for twenty years to build it. I am not sure about the numbers, but it was a gigantic undertaking. It was built as the Pharaoh's tomb so that he would be remembered forever—the great Pharaoh that he was. You all, of course, remember him. That was Pharaoh . . . ah . . . Pharaoh . . . ah . . . who? Khufu. You remembered that, didn't you? My, did he go to a lot of trouble for nothing?

Then there was a fellow who built the largest structure ever built on this planet. He wasn't leaving any doubts about the fact that he would be remembered. It is the only manmade structure that can be seen from the moon—the Great Wall of China, which makes its way for 1,500 miles—a gigantic enterprise. That, of course, was built by the well known and famous . . . somebody help me. Who was it? The largest structure ever built by man. Surely, we remember him. Shih-Huang-Ti. You knew that, didn't you? It was just on the tip of your tongue.

Maybe it is not size that counts. Perhaps it is beauty. What is the most beautiful building that has ever been built? Probably the experts would pretty much agree that it is the Taj Mahal in northern India that Shah Jahan built for his beautiful wife, who died in childbirth. She would be remembered forever by the most magnificent, beautiful, gorgeous building ever built on this planet. I am sure none of us will ever forget her. Her name was . . . ah . . . ? What was her name again? Arjumand. You knew that, didn't you? It just wouldn't come up on your computer.

THE KING OF KINGS

British poet Percy Shelley, in one of his sonnets, tells of meeting a traveler from Egypt who, in a trek across the desert wasteland, came upon the remains of a marble statue. All that remained on the pedestal were two feet and the lower part of two gigantic legs. Some distance away, lying in the sand, was the cracked remnant of what had been the head. The visage thereof had a cruel sneer to the lips.

When the traveler rubbed the sand away from the pedestal, he found this inscription: "My name is Ozymandias, king of kings: Look on my works, ye mighty, and despair!" He turned and looked, and as far as the eye could see, there was nothing but the shifting sand, and yet Ozymandias took to himself the name of king of kings. However, whatever kingdom and glory he once realized had all disappeared.

The true King of kings was meek and lowly of mind, and came into Jerusalem on Palm Sunday riding on the colt of a donkey. Here was the King of kings and Lord of lords—the King of all creation.

The great historian, Will Durant, wrote a major series of books on the history of the Western World. The volume, which covered a period when Rome was in her glory, is titled *Caesar and Christ*. Is it not astonishing that in writing of that period he would place next to Caesar, the ruler of the world, the name of an itinerant peasant preacher from a conquered backwater called Palestine? Yet that peasant was, indeed, and is, the King of kings and has outlived the Caesars and the empire which crucified Him.

Jesus is the Eternal King of kings, the One with whom there dwelt all supremacy. Our true significance in life comes through following and serving Him. That which we do for Him will last forever.

LASTING REMEMBRANCE

It seems that such things as stone memorials are not likely to cause us to have any real lasting remembrance or significance. Perhaps you are one of those who believes in immortality through the memory of your family. Yet I wonder how many of you reading this remember the first and last name of your *maternal* great grandmother. I don't, and I venture to say that 10 or 15 percent of you might, but that's about all.

How fleeting is life, and how soon the waves come in and wipe away all of the footprints. If we are going to find real and lasting significance, influence, and remembrance in this world, it is not going to be in the things of flesh, all of which will perish. A million years from now, all of these things will be long gone and forgotten, for Christ said, "That which is born of the flesh is flesh [and like flesh it molders and crumbles into dust], and that which is born of the Spirit is spirit" (John 3:6). Christ is that One who says, "Behold, I make all things new" (Revelation 21:5).

The Greek term used for "new" is one of several that could have been used, but the word used here means it is actually newer every day. Christ made me new more than fifty years ago. I'm newer today than I was yesterday, and I'll be newer tomorrow. Paul says, "Even though our outward man is perishing, yet the inward man is being renewed day by day" (2 Corinthians 4:16). The things of the Spirit last forever.

Dwight L. Moody said, "Work with souls, for they alone will last forever." Yes, my friends, if you would have an eternal significance, if you would make a difference that will last forever, if you want to have real significance for life, do it as God says. Do it according to His Word. Be concerned for those things that God is concerned for.

NEW LIFE IN CHRIST

The Bible declares, "Therefore, if anyone is in Christ, he is a new creation; old things have passed away; behold, all things have become new" (2 Corinthians 5:17). This is the wonder of Jesus Christ that makes all things new. Many years ago I received an emergency call from a man in Ohio who said that he *had* to see me. It was imperative. I told him I would be glad to see him and made an appointment. He flew down with his wife from Ohio to Ft. Lauderdale, came into my office, and told me this remarkable story.

He said that he had lived his entire life for but one purpose, and that was sin. It didn't matter what kind of sin; he was interested in it all, whether it was drugs, alcohol, sex, or thievery. He even told me some things worse than that. He said he had been an alcoholic, a drunk, for years. In fact, it got so bad that he finally got drunk every night of his life. He managed to stay sober (reasonably so) long enough to work during the day, but finally it got so bad that he lost his job.

Most people would be really depressed if they lost their job. He rejoiced. He was delighted. That meant he could get drunk all day and all night—which he did. He had ten thousand dollars saved and he soon drank it all down. When that was gone, he mortgaged his home and drank all of that.

Of course, during all of these thirty years, he had reproached his wife daily, cursed and beat her and their children and was, indeed, a miserable miscreant of a human being, if ever there was one. He began to get terrible headaches about once every week. They were so bad he would roll around and beat his head on the floor. He finally decided it must be his teeth causing the headaches, so he went to the dentist. The dentist x-rayed his teeth and told him there was nothing at all wrong with them. He said, "Pull them all out."

The dentist said, "That is ridiculous. There is nothing wrong with your teeth." He insisted, and finally, reluctantly, the dentist pulled out every one of his teeth—and the headaches got worse, until now he was having them every day.

One day, in his misery, he was up at one o'clock in the morning going through the TV channels. He came across *The Coral Ridge Hour*. Something I said stopped him, and he didn't change the channel. It was a sermon titled "Amazing Grace." He listened to it, and his attention was riveted by the concept of grace—that there actually was a God who could help him.

He didn't believe that for sure, but it was certainly worth thinking about. He decided after that to go ice fishing up in Ohio. He went in the middle of the winter to a lake, carved a hole in the ten-inch thick ice, dropped a couple of lines in, and waited. He waited for an hour or more and there wasn't a bite. It was one-thirty and—recalling what I said—he said, "Lord Jesus Christ, if you're up there, I want to catch a two to three pound wall-eyed pike by three o'clock." Two-thirty, not a bite. Two forty-five, not a bite. Two fifty-five, not a bite. He pulled up one of the lines, wrapped it up, and set it aside. Two fifty-nine, not a bite.

Three o'clock. He picked up the other line and started pulling it up and instantly, he had a strike. He looked at his watch again. It was exactly three o'clock. He got so excited he started pulling the line in, and the line broke. He couldn't believe it. He stood there staring down into the hole with the broken end of the line in his hand, and he thought, "I thought this was an answer to prayer."

Then he noticed a green line coming up out of the hole and running down the ice. He fell to his knees, pulled off his gloves, and tried to dig it out. It was frozen in the ice. He finally got the line free and started pulling again. The fish was still on the line. He pulled the fish more, and more, and more until its nose came out of the water—and the line broke a second time and went right into the water, and the fish disappeared.

He was totally confused and also quite skeptical. As he stood there looking down into that water, suddenly the fish floated to the surface. It must be dead, he thought, and he reached down and grabbed it. It was very much alive, but it had floated to the surface. Lo and behold, it was a pike—a wall-eyed pike, which was very rarely caught in that lake. He took it home and weighed it. It weighed exactly three pounds. Pike, wall-eyed pike, three pounds, exactly three o'clock, line breaks twice! This has to be a supernatural work . . . and his life was totally changed.

No, it wasn't. If you think that, you don't know what a problem humankind really has. You don't know what depravity means. He started drinking more. The headaches got even worse. One night he was rolling around on the floor, foaming at the mouth, pounding his head on the floor. He looked across the room in desperation and saw his gun case. He dragged himself across the room on the floor, reached up, and pulled out his pistol. He checked it to make sure all of the barrels were loaded, and put it up to his forehead with his thumb on the trigger. He began to squeeze.

Then he remembered something. That preacher at one o'clock in the morning had said that Christ could make all things new. He cried out, "O Christ, make me new!" *Instantly* he was changed. He looked at the gun in wonderment, put it down, and got up. That afternoon, when his wife came in from work, he was standing there with tears just dripping off his face. His wife looked at him in shock, and he said, "Don't worry, dear, I won't hurt you. I have become a new man in Christ." His wife was led to the Lord. The two of them joined a church. He got a job making twice as much as he had made before. They became active members of the church and for five years served Christ in that church.

When I first told this story to my congregation several years ago, I said: "I'm sure some of you are thinking, 'Where do you find those stories? Do you have a book of preacher's fantastic sermons or something?'"

I went on to say, "No. If there is a couple in this sanctuary whose lives I have described in the minutest detail, whose experiences I have very accurately portrayed, would you please stand?" These two people from Ohio stood up as *prima facia* evidence that Jesus Christ's Word is true: "Behold, I make all things new" (Revelation 21:5). "Therefore, if anyone is in Christ, he is a new creation; old things have passed away; behold, all things have become new" (2 Corinthians 5:17).

Consider Jacob DeShazer. He was a pilot in World War II. He flew with Lt. Col. James H. Doolittle when they bombed Tokyo. In a later mission he was shot down, captured by the Japanese, and put in a Japanese prison, where he was regularly tortured by his jailers. He lived for just one purpose. He had a burning, bitter, intense, white-hot hatred for everything Japanese, and he lived only for the day when he could get his hands around the throat of these tormentors and crush the life out of them.

One day he came across a copy of the New Testament. Jacob DeShazer read that, and he read the part where it said that Christ could make people new. Jesus Christ came into his life when he placed his trust in Him, and he asked Him to come and help him and change him. His life was transformed, and that hatred was replaced by a love for the Japanese—so much so that when he finally got home and out of the Air Force, he became a missionary.

Where did he go? He returned to Japan. He wrote out his experience in a little tract, and it was distributed in Japan. One day someone was distributing the tract in one of the great train stations in Tokyo. One was handed to a very dejected man—a man who had lost all meaning and purpose for life, a man who had had a great dream of a glorious Japan that would conquer the world and bring in a golden era of peace. He would be a part of that, but now the war was over, and he was utterly destroyed. They had lost. It had all been in vain. Now there was nothing to look forward to. Everything had crumbled for him.

He had once been a national hero. You may remember his name. It was Mitsuo Fuchida, of *Tora, Tora, Tora*. This was the code word (literally translated "Tiger, Tiger, Tiger") and meant, "All squadrons attack." Captain Fuchida was the commander who led 360 planes that came screaming out of the sky with their loads of death and destroyed Pearl Harbor. When the smoke cleared and the sun set that day on Pearl Harbor, more American sailors had been killed than in the entire World War I—and Mitsuo Fuchida was a national hero in Japan. Later, it was all over and they were a conquered people. There was no hope, no purpose, no significance, and no future for him.

His eyes fell on the words written by Jacob DeShazer, a prisoner of the Japanese. He read of the transformation that took place in this man's life, and Mitsuo Fuchida cried out to Christ to come and change his life. His life also was transformed and he, too, became an evangelist. Mitsuo Fuchida and Jacob DeShazer teamed up to become an evangelistic pair, and they preached great crusades to thousands of Japanese all over those islands. The grace of God can cause all things to be changed. "Old things have passed away; behold, all things have become new" (2 Corinthians 5:17b). They both saw a kingdom that has no end—a kingdom that has an everlasting significance.

Yes, there is something worth living for. There is something that will give eternal significance to life, and that is the kingdom of God. Christ said, "But seek first the kingdom of God and His righteousness, and all these things shall be added to you" (Matthew 6:33). If you want a significance that will not be as fleeting as those footprints in the sand, then pay attention to the words of Daniel, the wise prophet of the Old Testament, who said,

> Those who are wise shall shine
> Like the brightness of the firmament,
> And those who turn many to righteousness
> Like the stars forever and ever (Daniel 12:3).

SIGNIFICANCE FOREVER AND EVER

Do you want to have significance forever? Would you like to be a star forever? We have all kinds of stars in this world: movie stars, football stars, TV stars, basketball stars, and rock stars. Most of them are shooting stars, but you can be a star forever and ever. Who are going to be the stars in that eternal kingdom? Those who turn many to righteousness. Ah, dear friend, we need to become concerned with the things that concern almighty God. How many people take their trek down the beach, leaving their footprints in sand, with no concern other than their own business, their own home, their own advancement— nothing but "me, my, and mine"? They have not a moment's thought or concern for those things that concerned God and His Son Jesus and caused Him to come and give His life. "For the Son of Man has come to seek and to save that which was lost" (Luke 19:10).

Are His concerns your concerns? Is His passion your passion? The stars in Heaven will precisely be those for whom that is true. God's passion is their passion. God has created them, and in Him they live and move and have their being. Every breath they take is from Him. He has provided for their needs throughout all the years of their lives. He has told them they are going to come before Him. He has sent His Son to die for them in order that they might be used as His ambassadors plenipotentiary.

This passage in 2 Corinthians goes on to say: "Now then, we are ambassadors for Christ, as though God were pleading through us: we implore you on Christ's behalf, be reconciled to God" (2 Corinthians 5:20). If you have been saved, you have been saved to be an ambassador for Christ. Are you? Do you represent the throne of Heaven, the King of glory? Do you represent Him before others? Do you tell His will and desires for their lives to them? Do you share that Gospel with others?

Don't be so shortsighted as to think that you will find your significance in this world, because I assure you that the waves of time will wash it all away. It will be as though you had never been. Though your monument be as tall as a pyramid, as long as the Great Wall of China, or as beautiful as the Taj Mahal, you will be forgotten. Oh, that you might grasp why God has you in this world, while still there is time.

Furthermore, we should use our gifts for God's glory. If someone is called to be an artist, let him be an artist to the glory of God. That doesn't necessarily mean the plan of salvation needs to be tucked away in some part of the painting. Johann Sebastian Bach wrote every note to the glory of Jesus Christ, yet not every single one of this great composer's works were directly Christian, although most of them are. Bach had written at the top of each sheet of music: S.D.G., short for the Latin *Soli Deo Gloria*—to God alone be the glory.

One time a lady with a record album met with the manager of a Christian radio station. She said to him, "When the Lord calls you to do something, He doesn't necessarily tell you to do it well. He just says to do it." Needless to say, the album was not very good. I must differ with that dear lady. We have a motto at our church: "Excellence in all things, and all things to God's glory." I hope more and more Christians will adopt a similar attitude. Jesus spared nothing in paying the price for our redemption. Therefore, we should honor Him with our best.

Soli Deo Gloria.

NOTES

1 Write to me: James Kennedy, Box 40, Ft. Lauderdale, Fla. 33302 and ask for *Beginning Again* or call 800-988-7884.

2 Saint Bernard of Clairvaux, "O Sacred Head, Now Wounded," in Donald P. Hustad, ed., *Hymns for the Living Church* (Carol Stream, Ill.: Hope Publishing Co., 1974/1984), #136.

3 Lee Strobel, *Inside the Mind of Unchurched Harry and Mary: How to Reach Friends and Family Who Avoid God and the Church* (Grand Rapids: Zondervan, 1993), 36-37.

4 Peter Stoner, *Science Speaks* (Chicago: Moody Press, 1963), 109. Quoted in Josh McDowell, *Evidence That Demands a Verdict* (San Bernardino, Calif.: Campus Crusade for Christ, 1972), 167.

5 Strobel, *Inside the Mind of Unchurched Harry and Mary*, 37.

6 Ibid., 36.

7 Kenneth Woodward, "2000 Years of Jesus," *Newsweek*, 29 March, 1999, 52, 54.

8 Cecil F. Alexander, "There Is a Green Hill Far Away," 1848, in Hustad, ed., *Hymns for the Living Church*, #138.

9 Saint Bernard of Clairvaux, "Jesus, the Very Thought of Thee," Hustad, ed., *Hymns of the Living Church*, #83.

10 Rabbi Daniel Lapin, quoted in sermon from D. James Kennedy, *What If Jesus Had Never Been Born?* (Fort Lauderdale: Coral Ridge Ministries, 2001).

11 Allan Bloom, *The Closing of the American Mind* (New York: Simon & Schuster, 1987), 25.

12 Paul Johnson, *Modern Times: From the Twenties to the Nineties* (New York: Harper Collins, 1991), 4.

13 Earl D. Radmacher, gen. ed., *The Nelson Study Bible* (Nashville: Thomas Nelson Publishers, 1997), 1627 (note on 26:53).

14 To see just how severe it was for the Jews in 70 A.D., when the Romans conquered them once and for all, see the writings of Eusebius and Josephus. Co-author Jerry Newcombe has culled the most terrifying aspects of that conquest in Chapter 11 of his book, *Coming Again* (Colorado Springs, Colo.: Chariot Victor, 1999).

15 John Foxe, *Foxe's Book of Martyrs*, in updated English by Jerry Newcombe, ed., "The Deaths of the Apostles," in *The Moral of the Story: Timeless Tales to Cherish & Share* (Nashville: Broadman & Holman, 1996), 63.

16 Scriptures referred to for this chapter are Matthew 27, Luke 23, and John 18, 19.

17 Thomas Arnold, *Sermons on the Christian Life: Its Hopes, Its Fears, Its Close*, sixth edition (London: T. Fellowes, 1859), 324.

18 Josh McDowell, *Evidence That Demands a Verdict* (San Bernardino, Calif.: Campus Crusade for Christ, 1972), 209.

19 Quoted in ibid., 214.

20 Ibid., 223.

21 Ibid.

22 Transcript from a TV interview with Jerry Newcombe, Ft. Lauderdale, Fla., Spring 1988.

23 McDowell, *Evidence That Demands a Verdict*, 179.

24 Hill's *Lectures in Divinity*, Vol. I, 47, 48. Quoted in William Taylor, *The Miracles of Our Saviour* (New York: Hodder and Stoughton, 1890), 21-22.

25 McDowell, *Evidence That Demands a Verdict*, 233.

26 Ibid., 244.

27 Ibid., 248-255.

28 One of the reasons he came to believe this was because it says in John 5:2, "Now there *is* in Jerusalem by the Sheep Gate a pool . . ." [emphasis mine] When the Roman general Titus came in 70 A.D., he thoroughly destroyed Jerusalem and much of Israel. So Robinson believed, therefore, that John, the final Gospel, was written before 70 A.D.

29 Gary Habermas, *The Historical Jesus: Ancient Evidence for the*

Life of Christ (Joplin, Mo., College Press Publishing Company, 1996), 187-228.

30 See Mike Licona, *Cross Examined* (Virginia Beach, Va.: TruthQuest Publishers, 1999).

31 D. James Kennedy and Jerry Newcombe, *What If Jesus Had Never Been Born?* (Nashville: Thomas Nelson Publishers, 1994), 178.

32 See Pierre Barbet, *A Doctor At Calvary: The Passion of Our Lord Jesus Christ as Described by a Surgeon*, trans. by the Earl of Wicklow (New York: P.J. Kenedy & Sons, 1953).

33 Some scholars say Jesus was crucified in 33 A.D. That is still after this Pontius Pilate coin was minted.

34 Quoted in John C. Iannone, "Credibly Discrediting the Carbon-14 Test on the Shroud," in *The Mystery of the Shroud of Turin* (Staten Island, NY: Alba House, 1998), 168.

35 Ibid., 169.

36 Mary and Alan Whanger, *The Shroud of Turin: An Adventure of Discovery* (Franklin, Tenn.: Providence House Publishers, 1998), 105, 107.

37 Marc Antonacci, *The Resurrection of the Shroud: New Scientific, Medical and Archaeological Evidence* (New York: M. Evans and Company, Inc., 2000), 157.

38 David Van Biema, "Science and the Shroud," *TIME*, 20 April, 1998, 61.

39 Ibid.

40 Ian Wilson, *The Turin Shroud* (Middlesex, England: Penguin Books, 1978).

41 Antonacci, *The Resurrection of the Shroud*, 8-9.

42 Van Biema, "Science and the Shroud," 57.

43 The shorter catechism of the Westminster Confession of Faith.

INDEX